The American Novel
Sinclair Lewis to the Present

GOLDENTREE BIBLIOGRAPHIES
In Language and Literature
under the series editorship of
O. B. Hardison, Jr.

The American Novel

Sinclair Lewis to the Present

compiled by

Blake Nevius

University of California, Los Angeles

AHM Publishing Corporation
Northbrook, Illinois 60062

ISBN: 0-88295-524-1
(Formerly 390-66671-8)

Library of Congress Card Number: 76-103094

PRINTED IN THE UNITED STATES OF AMERICA
783
Second Printing

Preface

THE FOLLOWING BIBLIOGRAPHY is intended for graduate and advanced undergraduate students in courses on the contemporary American novel and related subjects. Designed as a convenient guide to scholarship and criticism in the field, the listing is necessarily selective. Although 48 individual novelists are included, the student may regret certain omissions—for example, John Cheever, Herbert Gold, Paul Bowles, or James Purdy. Such omissions reflect not so much a judgment on the compiler's part as a dearth of extended or serious commentary on these novelists and, incidentally, the degree to which studies of the contemporary American novel have concentrated on a half dozen writers.

In order to keep this bibliography to a practical size, it has been necessary to omit a number of references: unpublished dissertations, literary histories (except for a very few), most bibliographies of bibliography, and short notes and explications (except when they contain important data or comment). Although book reviews are not included, the listing does contain a number of important review-articles.

In general, the compiler has attempted to steer a middle course between the brief lists of references included in the average textbook and the long professional bibliography in which significant items are often lost in the sheer number of references given. This bibliography should materially assist the student in his effort to survey a topic, write reports and term papers, prepare for examinations, and do independent reading. Attention is called to four features intended to enhance its utility.

(1) Extra margin on each page permits listing of library call numbers of often used items.

(2) Extra space at the bottom of every other page permits inclusion of additional entries.

(3) An index by author follows the bibliography proper.

(4) The index and cross-reference numbers direct the reader to the page and position-on-the-page of the desired entry. Thus, in an entry such as

KLEIN, Marcus. "James Baldwin: A Question of Identity." See 6.13,

the number 6.13 indicates that the entry referred to is on page 6, and is the 13th item on that page. Both page numbers and individual entry numbers are conspicuous in size and position so that the process of finding entries is fast as well as simple.

Annotations which may conclude an individual entry are as follows: (1) cross-reference(s) to other entries in the bibliography in which the work cited is also included; (2) an explicatory phrase describing the subject of an allusive title; and (3) abbreviations, in brackets, of paperback publishers and series numbers given in *Paperbound Books in Print*.

Symbols for journals cited follow the standard forms given in the Table of Symbols at the beginning of recent *PMLA* bibliographies. The symbols and their meanings are as follows:

ABC	*American Book Collector*
Accent	
AI	*American Imago*
AL	*American Literature*
AMer	*American Mercury*
Anglica	
AnRev	*Anchor Review*
APref	*American Prefaces*
AQ	*American Quarterly*
AR	*Antioch Review*
ARev	*American Review*
ArQ	*Arizona Quarterly*
AS	*American Speech*
ASch	*American Scholar*
Atlantic	
Audit	
BAASB	*British Association for American Studies Bulletin*
BB	*Bulletin of Bibliography*
BNYPL	*Bulletin of the New York Public Library*
Bookman	
BSTCF	*Ball State Teachers College Forum*
BSUF	*Ball State University Forum*
BuR	*Bucknell Review*
BUSE	*Boston University Studies in English*
BuUS	*Bucknell University Studies*
CarQ	*Carolina Quarterly*
CaSE	*Carnegie Series in English*
CathW	*Catholic World*

CE	*College English*
CEEAL	*Critical Essays in English and American Literature*
CEJ	*California English Journal*
CentR	*The Centennial Review* (Michigan State Univ.)
Century	
CF	*Canadian Forum*
ChiR	*Chicago Review*
ChS	*Christian Scholar*
CJ	*Classical Journal*
CJF	*Chicago Jewish Forum*
CL	*Comparative Literature*
CLAJ	*College Language Association Journal* (Morgan State Coll., Baltimore)
ClareQ	*Claremont Quarterly* (Claremont, Calif.)
CLS	*Comparative Literature Studies* (Univ. of Maryland)
CM	*Carleton Miscellany*
Colophon	
ColQ	*Colorado Quarterly*
Commentary	
Confluence	
CRAS	*The Centennial Review of Arts and Science* (Michigan State Univ.)
Crit	*Critique: Studies in Modern Fiction*
Criticism (Wayne State Univ.)	
CritQ	*Critical Quarterly*
CrR	*Creative Reading*
CUF	*Columbia University Forum*
CurH	*Current History*
DD	*Double Dealer*
Dial	
DQ	*Delphian Quarterly*
E & S	*Essays and Studies by Members of the English Association*
Ebony	
EdL	*Etudes de Lettres* (Univ. de Lausanne)
EIE	*English Institute Essays*
EJ	*English Journal*
ELH	*Journal of English Literary History*
Encounter (London)	
Epoch	
ER	*Evergreen Review*
ES	*English Studies*
Esquire	
Fact	
FaS	*Faulkner Studies*
Folio	
FQ	*Four Quarters*
GaR	*Georgia Review*
GR	*Germanic Review*
H & H	*Hound & Horn*
Harpers	

HC	*The Hollins Critic* (Hollins Coll., Va.)
Hispania (Univ. of Massachusetts)	
HLB	*Harvard Library Bulletin*
Holiday	
HoR	*Hopkins Review*
Horizon	
HudR	*Hudson Review*
Interim	
IntL	*International Literature*
JA	*Jahrbuch für Amerikastudien*
JAAC	*Journal of Aesthetics and Art Criticism*
JASP	*Journal of Abnormal and Social Psychology*
JEGP	*Journal of English and Germanic Philology*
KR	*Kenyon Review*
L&L	*Life & Letters*
L&LT	*Life & Letters Today*
L&P	*Literature and Psychology* (Univ. of Massachusetts)
LHR	*Lock Haven Review* (Lock Haven State Coll., Pa.)
Life	
LoM	*London Mercury*
LSUSHS	*Louisiana State University Studies, Humanities Series*
Mainstream	
Mandrake	
MAQR	*Michigan Alumnus Quarterly Review*
MFS	*Modern Fiction Studies*
Midstream	
Midway	
MissQ	*Mississippi Quarterly*
MJ	*Midwest Journal*
MLN	*Modern Language Notes*
ModM	*Modern Monthly*
ModQ	*Modern Quarterly*
MQ	*Midwest Quarterly* (Pittsburg, Kan.)
MR	*Massachusetts Review* (Univ. of Massachusetts)
NAR	*North American Review*
Nation	
NCHR	*North Carolina Historical Review*
NEQ	*New England Quarterly*
NewC	*New Colophon*
NewL	*New Leader*
NewM	*New Masses*
NewR	*New Republic*
NLB	*Newberry Library Bulletin*
NMQ	*New Mexico Quarterly*
NMQR	*New Mexico Quarterly Review*
NR	*Northwest Review*
NYTBR	*New York Times Book Review*
OUR	*Ohio University Review* (Athens, O.)
ParisR	*Paris Review*
PAW	*Princeton Alumni Weekly*

PBSA	Papers of the Bibliographical Society of America
PELL	Papers on English Language and Literature (Southern Illinois Univ.)
Perspective (Washington Univ.)	
Perspectives USA	
Phoenix (Coll. of Charleston, S.C.)	
Phylon	
Playboy	
PMASAL	*Papers of the Michigan Academy of Science, Arts, and Letters*
PMLA	*Publications of the Modern Language Association of America*
PR	*Partisan Review*
PrS	*Prairie Schooner*
PS	*Pacific Spectator*
PsyR	*Psychoanalytic Review*
PULC	*Princeton University Library Chronicle*
QQ	*Queen's Quarterly*
QRL	*Quarterly Review of Literature* (Bard Coll.)
REL	*Review of English Literature* (Leeds)
Renascence	
Reporter	
RIP	*Rice Institute Pamphlets*
RLM	*La Revue des Lettres Modernes*
RLV	*Revue des Langues Vivantes* (Bruxelles)
RusR	*Russian Review*
SA	*Studi Americani* (Roma)
S&S	*Science and Society*
SAQ	*South Atlantic Quarterly*
SatR	*Saturday Review*
SatRL	*Saturday Review of Literature*
SB	*Studies in Bibliography: Papers of the Bibliographical Society of the University of Virginia*
Scrutiny	
SDR	*South Dakota Review*
SeA	*Seven Arts*
SEJ	*Southern Economic Journal*
SFQ	*Southern Folklore Quarterly*
Shenandoah	
SoR	*Southern Review* (Louisiana State Univ.)
SovL	*Soviet Literature*
SR	*Sewanee Review*
SSF	*Studies in Short Fiction* (Newberry Coll., S.C.)
Story	
Studies (Dublin)	
SWR	*Southwest Review*
Symposium	
TamR	*Tamarack Review* (Toronto)
TAY	*Twice A Year*
TC	*Twentieth Century*
TCL	*Twentieth Century Literature*

TexSE	*Texas Studies in English*
TFSB	*Tennessee Folklore Society Bulletin*
Thought	
TQ	*Texas Quarterly* (Univ. of Texas)
TriQ	*Tri-Quarterly* (Evanston, Ill.)
TSE	*Tulane Studies in English*
TSL	*Tennessee Studies in Literature*
TSLL	*Texas Studies in Literature and Language*
UKCR	*University of Kansas City Review*
UMPAW	University of Minnesota Pamphlets on American Writers
UR	*University Review* (Kansas City, Mo.)
UTQ	*University of Toronto Quarterly*
UTR	*University of Toronto Review*
UVM	*University of Virginia Magazine*
VQR	*Virginia Quarterly Review*
Wake	
WHR	*Western Humanities Review*
WR	*Western Review*
WSCL	*Wisconsin Studies in Contemporary Literature*
XUS	*Xavier University Studies*
YFS	*Yale French Studies*
YR	*Yale Review*
YULG	*Yale University Library Gazette*

Note: *The publisher and compiler invite suggestions for additions to future editions of the bibliography.*

Contents

The entries under the individual novelists are generally arranged in the following sub-categories:

TEXTS
BIBLIOGRAPHY
BIOGRAPHICAL AND CRITICAL BOOKS
BIOGRAPHICAL AND CRITICAL ESSAYS

Bibliographies

1 *American Literature.* Quarterly journal of scholarship and criticism published since 1929. Durham, N.C.: Duke Univ. Press. [Each issue contains "Articles on American Literature Appearing in Current Periodicals," prepared by the Bibliography Committee of the American Literature Section of the Modern Language Association.]

2 COAN, Otis W. and Richard G. LILLARD. *America in Fiction: An Annotated List of Novels That Interpret Aspects of Life in the United States.* 4th ed. Stanford, Calif.: Stanford Univ. Press, 1956.

3 GERSTENBERGER, Donna and George HENDRICK. *The American Novel 1789–1959: A Checklist of Twentieth-Century Criticism.* Denver, Col.: Alan Swallow, 1961. [41-Swall]

4 GOHDES, Clarence. *Bibliographical Guide to the Study of the Literature of the U.S.A.* 2nd ed. Durham, N.C.: Duke Univ. Press, 1964.

5 JONES, Howard Mumford and Richard M. LUDWIG. *Guide to American Literature and Its Backgrounds Since 1890.* 3rd ed. Cambridge, Mass.: Harvard Univ. Press, 1964. [HUP]

6 LEARY, Lewis G. *Articles on American Literature 1900–1950.* Durham, N.C.: Duke Univ. Press, 1954.

7 MILLETT, Fred B., ed. *Contemporary American Authors.* New York: Harcourt, Brace, 1944. [Critical survey and over 200 bio-bibliographies; dated but still useful.]

8 *MLA International Bibliography of Books and Articles on the Modern Languages and Literatures.* Published each May as an annual supplement to *PMLA.* [Each issue lists scholarly and critical works of the preceding year.]

9 SPILLER, Robert E., Willard THORP, Thomas H. JOHNSON, Henry S. CANBY, and Richard M. LUDWIG, eds. *Literary History of the United States: Bibliography.* 3rd ed., rev. New York: Macmillan, 1963.

10 WHITEMAN, Maxwell. *A Century of Fiction by American Negroes, 1853–1952: A Descriptive Bibliography.* Philadelphia: [the author], 1955.

11 WOODRESS, James, ed. *American Literary Scholarship: An Annual/1963.* Durham, N.C.: Duke Univ. Press, 1965, and annually since. [Each volume has essays by various authors evaluating the year's work on individual authors and topics, including Faulkner, Hemingway, Fitzgerald, Fiction: 1900–1930, and Fiction: 1930 to the present.] [Duke]

Reference Works

1 HART, James D. *The Oxford Companion to American Literature.* 4th ed. New York: Oxford Univ. Press, 1965.

2 HERZBERG, Max, Jr., ed. *The Reader's Encyclopedia of American Literature.* New York: Crowell, 1962.

3 KUNITZ, Stanley J. and Howard HAYCRAFT, eds. *Twentieth Century Authors.* New York: H. W. Wilson, 1944.

4 KUNITZ, Stanley J., ed. *Twentieth Century Authors: First Supplement.* New York: H. W. Wilson, 1955.

5 WARFEL, Harry R. *American Novelists of Today.* New York: American Book, 1951.

American Literary History

6 BRADBURY, John M. *Renaissance in the South: A Critical History of the Literature, 1920–1960.* Chapel Hill, N.C.: Univ. of North Carolina Press, 1963. [Useful for its survey of minor southern novelists.]

7 CARGILL, Oscar. *Intellectual America: Ideas on the March.* New York: Macmillan, 1941.

8 COWLEY, Malcolm. *Exile's Return.* New York: Viking, 1951. [Account, by a participant, of the expatriate movement after World War I.] [C4 Comp]

9 HICKS, Granville. *The Great Tradition: An Interpretation of American Literature Since the Civil War.* Rev. ed. New York: Macmillan, 1935. [A Marxist interpretation.]

10 HORTON, Rod W. and Herbert W. EDWARDS. *Backgrounds of American Literary Thought.* 2nd ed. New York: Appleton-Century-Crofts, 1967. [Appl]

11 HOWARD, Leon. *Literature and the American Tradition.* Garden City, N.Y.: Doubleday, 1960. [A329-Anch]

12 KAZIN, Alfred. *On Native Grounds.* New York: Reynal & Hitchcock, 1942. [A69-Anch]

13 LOGGINS, Vernon. *I Hear America: Literature in the United States Since 1900.* New York: Crowell, 1937.

14 SPILLER, Robert E., *et al.* eds. *Literary History of the United States.* Rev. ed. New York: Macmillan, 1963.

15 THORP, Willard. *American Writing in the Twentieth Century.* Cambridge, Mass.: Harvard Univ. Press, 1960.

The Novel as a Form

1 BEACH, Joseph Warren. *The Twentieth-Century Novel: Studies in Technique.* New York: Century, 1932.

2 BOOTH, Wayne C. *The Rhetoric of Fiction.* Chicago: Univ. of Chicago Press, 1961. [Chi]

3 DE VOTO, Bernard. *The World of Fiction.* Boston: Houghton Mifflin, 1950.

4 EDEL, Leon. *The Modern Psychological Novel.* New York: Grossett & Dunlap, 1964. [Originally published, before revision, as *The Psychological Novel, 1900–1950.*] [Evergreen-E134]

5 FORSTER, E. M. *Aspects of the Novel.* New York: Harcourt, Brace, 1927. [HB19-Harv]

6 FRIEDMAN, Melvin J. *Stream of Consciousness: A Study in Literary Method.* New Haven, Conn.: Yale Univ. Press, 1955.

7 FRIEDMAN, Norman. "Point of View in Fiction: The Development of a Critical Concept." *PMLA*, LXX (1955), 1160–1184. [Considers, among others, Hemingway and Fitzgerald.]

8 LESSER, Simon O. "The Functions of Form in Narrative Art." *Psychiatry*, XVIII (1955), 51–63. Also in 10.19.

9 LEVIN, Harry. *Symbolism and Fiction.* Charlottesville, Va.: Univ. of Virginia Press, 1956.

10 LUBBOCK, Percy. *The Craft of Fiction.* New York: Scribner, 1921. [A brilliant defense of Jamesian theories of the well-made novel.] [C31-Comp]

11 LUKÁCS, Georg. *Realism in Our Time: Literature and the Class Struggle.* Trans. by John and Necke Mauder. "World Perspectives, Vol. XXXIII." New York: Harper & Row, 1964. [Perhaps the outstanding application of Marxist theory to the novel.]

12 MUIR, Edwin. *The Structure of the Novel.* London: Hogarth, 1928.

13 MULLER, Herbert J. *Modern Fiction: A Study of Values.* New York: Funk & Wagnall, 1937. [43994-McGH]

14 RAHV, Philip. "Fiction and the Criticism of Fiction." *The Myth and the Powerhouse.* New York: Farrar, Straus & Giroux, 1965, 33–60. [N291-Noon]

15 RANSOM, John Crowe. "The Understanding of Fiction." *KR*, XII (1950), 189–218. [Essay-review of Philip Rahv's *Image and Idea.*]

16 SCHOLES, Robert and Robert KELLOGG. *The Nature of Narrative.* New York: Oxford Univ. Press, 1966.

1 SCHOLES, Robert, ed. *Approaches to the Novel: Materials for a Poetics.* San Francisco, Calif.: Chandler Publishing, 1961. [Essays by various hands.] [CPC]

2 SCHORER, Mark. "Fiction and the 'Matrix of Analogy'." *KR*, XI (1949), 539–560.

3 SCHORER, Mark. "Technique as Discovery." *HudR*, I (1948), 67–87. Also in 4.1 and 13.15.

4 TATE, Allen. "Techniques of Fiction." *SR*, LII (1944), 210–225. Also in 13.15.

5 TRILLING, Lionel. "Manners, Morals and the Novel." *KR*, X (1947), 11–27. Also in 4.1 and 13.15.

6 WARREN, Austin and René WELLEK. "The Nature and Modes of Fiction." *The Theory of Literature.* New York: Harcourt, Brace, 1949. [HB22-Harv]

Histories of the American Novel

7 ALLEN, Walter. *The Modern Novel in Britain and the United States.* New York: Dutton, 1963. [D-167-Duttn]

8 CHASE, Richard. *The American Novel and Its Tradition.* Garden City, N.Y.: Doubleday, 1957. [A116-Anch]

9 FIEDLER, Leslie. *Love and Death in the American Novel.* New York: Criterion Books, 1960. [MG43-Mer]

10 HOFFMAN, Frederick J. *The Modern Novel in America: 1900–1950.* Chicago: Henry Regnery, 1951. [96035-Gate]

11 QUINN, Arthur Hobson. *American Fiction: An Historical and Critical Survey.* New York: Appleton-Century, 1936.

12 SNELL, George D. *The Shapers of American Fiction, 1798–1947.* New York: Dutton, 1947.

13 VAN DOREN, Carl. *The American Novel, 1789–1939.* New York Macmillan, 1940.

14 WAGENKNECHT, Edward. *Cavalcade of the American Novel.* New York: Henry Holt, 1952.

Special Studies of the American Novel

By Period

1   ALDRIDGE, John W. *After the Lost Generation: A Critical Study of the Writers of Two Wars.* New York: McGraw-Hill, 1951. [N118-Noon]

2   ALDRIDGE, John W. *Time to Murder and Create: The Contemporary Novel in Crisis.* New York: McKay, 1966.

3   BALDWIN, Charles C. *The Men Who Make Our Novels.* Rev. ed. New York: Dodd, Mead, 1924.

4   BAUMBACH, Jonathan. *The Landscape of Nightmare: Studies in the Contemporary American Novel.* New York: New York Univ. Press, 1965 (Orig.). [NYU]

5   BEACH, Joseph Warren. *American Fiction: 1920–1940.* New York: Macmillan, 1941.

6   BELLOW, Saul. *Recent American Fiction.* Washington, D.C.: Lib. of Congress, 1963. [A lecture.]

7   BOYNTON, Percy H. *America in Contemporary Fiction.* Chicago: Univ. of Chicago Press, 1940.

8   BURGESS, Anthony. "The Post-War American Novel: A View from the Periphery." *ASch*, XXXV (1966), 150–156.

9   BURKE, Kenneth. "A Decade of American Fiction." *Bookman*, LXIX (1929), 561–567.

10   COWLEY, Malcolm. *The Literary Situation.* New York: Viking, 1954. [C38-Comp]

11   COWLEY, Malcolm. "The Sense of Guilt." *KR*, XXVII (1965), 259–278. [American writing in the 1930's.]

12   DUFFEY, Bernard. *The Chicago Renaissance in American Letters.* Lansing, Mich.: Michigan State College Press, 1954.

13   EISINGER, Chester E. *Fiction of the Forties.* Chicago and London: Univ. of Chicago Press, 1963. [P188-Phoen.]

14   FLEISCHMANN, Wolfgang B. "A Look at the 'Beat Generation' Writers." *CarQ*, XI (1959), 13–20. Also in 14.10.

15   FRENCH, Warren. *The Social Novel at the End of an Era.* Carbondale and Edwardsville, Ill.: Univ. of Southern Illinois Press, 1966. [Fiction of the 1930's, esp. Faulkner, Steinbeck, Hemingway, Warren.]

16   FULLER, Edmund. *Man in Modern Fiction: Some Minority Opinions on Contemporary American Writing.* New York: Random House, 1958. [V177-Vin]

17   GEISMAR, Maxwell. *The Last of the Provincials: The American Novel, 1915–1925.* Boston: Houghton Mifflin, 1947. [Lewis, Cather, Anderson, Fitzgerald.] [AC45-Am Cen]

1 GEISMAR, Maxwell. *Writers in Crisis: The American Novel Between Two Wars.* Boston: Houghton Mifflin, 1942. [Lardner, Hemingway, Dos Passos, Faulkner, Wolfe, Steinbeck.] [AC38-Am Cen]

2 GOSSETT, Louise Y. *Violence in Recent Southern Fiction.* Durham, N.C.: Duke Univ. Press, 1965. [Caldwell, Wolfe, Faulkner, Warren, O'Connor, Welty, Styron, Capote, McCullers.]

3 HARTWICK, Harry. *The Foreground of American Fiction.* New York: American Book, 1934. [American fiction, 1890–1930.]

4 HASSAN, Ihab H. "The Character of Post-War Fiction in America." *EJ,* LI (1962), 1–8. Also in 14.10.

5 HATCHER, Harlan. *Creating the Modern American Novel.* New York: Farrar & Rinehart, 1935.

6 HAWKES, John, D. J. HUGHES, and Ihab H. HASSAN. "Symposium: Fiction Today." *MR,* III (1962), 784–797.

7 HICKS, Granville. "American Fiction Since the War." *EJ,* XXXVII (1948), 271–276.

8 HICKS, Granville. "Generations of the Fifties: Malamud, Gold, and Updike." See 12.17.

9 HOFFMAN, Frederick J. *The Art of Southern Fiction: A Study of Some Modern Novelists.* Carbondale, Ill.: Southern Illinois Univ. Press, 1967. (Capote, McCullers, O'Connor, Porter, Styron, Warren, Welty.)

10 HOFFMAN, Frederick J. *The Twenties: American Writing in the Postwar Decade.* Rev. ed. New York: Viking, 1962. [91478-Free P]

11 HYMAN, Stanley Edgar. "Some Trends in the Novel." *CE,* XX (1958), 1–9.

12 JOSEPHSON, Matthew. "The Young Generation: Its Young Novelists." *VQR,* IX (1933), 243–261.

13 KAZIN, Alfred. "The Alone Generation: A Comment on the Fiction of the Fifties." *Harper's,* CCXIX (Oct., 1959), 127–131. Also in 14.10.

14 KLEIN, Marcus. *After Alienation: American Novels in Mid-Century.* Cleveland and New York: World, 1964. [Bellow, Ellison, Baldwin, Morris, Malamud.] [M167-Mer]

15 LEWIS, R. W. B. "Recent Fiction: Picaro and Pilgrims." *A Time of Harvest.* Ed. by Robert E. Spiller. New York: Hill & Wang, 1962 (Orig.). [American fiction of the 1950's: Bellow, Purdy, Mailer.] [AC50-AmCen]

16 LUDWIG, Jack. *Recent American Novelists.* UMPAW No. 22. Minneapolis, Minn: Univ. of Minnesota Press, 1962. [UMP]

17 MICHAUD, Régis. *The American Novel Today: A Social and Psychological Study.* Boston: Little, Brown, 1928. [Lewis, Anderson, Cabell, and others.]

18 MIZENER, Arthur. "The Novel in America: 1920–1940." *Perspectives USA,* XV (Spring, 1956), 134–147.

19 O'FAOLAIN, Sean. "The Modern Novel." *VQR,* XI (1935), 339–351.

20 PARKINSON, Thomas, ed. *A Casebook on The Beat.* New York: Crowell, 1961. [Includes essays on Kerouac and Burroughs.] [TYC]

1 PODHORETZ, Norman. "The New Nihilism and the Novel." *PR*, XXV (1958), 576–590. Also in 6.21.

2 RUBIN, Louis D., Jr. *The Faraway Country: Writers of the Modern South.* Seattle, Wash.: Univ. of Washington Press, 1963. [Faulkner, Wolfe, Warren, Welty, Styron.] [WP-8-UWP]

3 SULLIVAN, Walter. "The Continuing Renascence: Southern Fiction in the Fifties." See 14.3.

4 SWADOS, Harvey. "The Image in the Mirror." *New World Writing* (12th Mentor Selection). New York: New American Library, 1957, 207–228. [A defense of the contemporary American novel.]

5 VAN DOREN, Carl. *Contemporary American Novelists, 1900–1920.* New York: Macmillan, 1922.

6 WALDMEIR, Joseph J. "Quest Without Faith." *Nation*, CXCIII (Nov. 18, 1961), 390–396. Also in 14.10. [American novelists after 1949.]

7 WIDMER, Kingsley. "The American Road: The Contemporary Novel." *UKCR*, XXVI (1960), 309–317. [Bellow, Malamud, Kerouac, Salinger, Algren, Gold.]

By Theme and Subject

8 ALBRECHT, W. P. "War and Fraternity: A Study of Some Recent American War Novels." *NMQ*, XXI (1952), 461–474.

9 ALDRIDGE, John W. "The War Writers Ten Years Later." See 13.12.

10 BARRETT, William. "American Fiction and American Values." *PR*, XVIII (1951), 681–690.

11 BEACH, Joseph Warren. "New Intentions in the Novel." *NAR*, CCXVIII (1923), 233–245.

12 BEACH, Joseph Warren. *The Outlook for American Prose.* Chicago: Univ. of Chicago Press, 1926.

13 BECKER, George J., ed. *Documents of Modern Literary Realism.* Princeton, N.J.: Princeton Univ. Press, 1963. [66-PUP]

14 BECKER, Stephen et al. "What's Wrong With the American Novel?" *ASch*, XXIV (1955), 464–503. [A forum, with contributions by Ellison, Styron, and Jean Stafford, among others.]

15 BELLOW, Saul. "The Jewish Writer and the English Literary Tradition." *Commentary*, VIII (1949), 366–367.

16 BELLOW, Saul. "Where Do We Go From Here: The Future of Fiction." *To the Young Writer: Hopwood Lectures, Second Series.* Ed. by A. L. Bader. Ann Arbor, Mich.: Univ. of Michigan Press, 1965, 136–146. Also in 21.3.

17 BLOTNER, Joseph. *The Modern American Political Novel, 1900–1960.* Austin, Tex.: Univ. of Texas Press, 1966. [PS18-RH]

18 BONE, Robert A. *The Negro Novel in America.* Rev. ed. New Haven, Conn.: Yale Univ. Press, 1965. [Y-149-Yale]

19 BOWDEN, Edwin T. *The Dungeon of the Heart: Human Isolation and the American Novel.* New York: Macmillan, 1961. [Includes Cather, Wolfe, Anderson, Faulkner, Steinbeck, Salinger.] [04872-Macm]

1 BRACE, Marjorie. "Thematic Problems of the American Novelist." *Accent*, VI (1945), 44–53. [Probes the failure of the modern American novelist.]

2 BRIDGMAN, Richard. *The Colloquial Style in America*. New York: Oxford Univ. Press, 1966. [Stein, Anderson, Lardner, Hemingway.]

3 BRUNEAU, Jean. "Existentialism and the American Novel." *YFS*, I (1948), 66–72.

4 BURGUM, Edwin Berry. *The Novel and the World's Dilemma*. New York: Oxford Univ. Press, 1947.

5 CHAPMAN, Arnold. *The Spanish American Reception of United States Fiction, 1920–1940*. UCPMP, No. 77. Berkeley, Calif.: Univ. of California Press, 1966.

6 COOPERMAN, Stanley. *World War I and the American Novel*. Baltimore, Md.: Johns Hopkins Press, 1967. [Cather, Dos Passos, Hemingway, Faulkner.]

7 COWLEY, Malcolm. " 'Not Men': A Natural History of American Naturalism." *KR*, IX (1947), 414–435.

8 CURLEY, Thomas F. "The Quarrel with Time in American Fiction." *ASch*, XXIX (1960), 552–560.

9 EISINGER, Chester E. "The American War Novel: An Affirming Flame." *PS*, IX (1955), 272–287.

10 ELLISON, Ralph. "The Negro Writer in America: An Exchange. II. Change the Joke and Slip the Yoke." *PR*, XXV (1958), 212–222.

11 ELLISON, Ralph. "Twentieth-Century Fiction and the Black Mask of Humanity." *Confluence*, II, iv (1953), 3–21.

12 ELLISON, Ralph. " 'A Very Stern Discipline': An Interview with Ralph Ellison." *Harpers* CCXXXIV (Mar., 1967), 76–95. [The Negro and Jewish writers' relation to American life and writing; the influences of Hemingway, Faulkner, and Wright.]

13 FARRELL, James T. "Social Themes in American Realism." *EJ*, XXXV (1946), 309–314.

14 FARRELL, James T. "Some Observations on Naturalism, So Called, in American Fiction." *AR*, X (1950), 247–264.

15 FEIED, Frederick. *No Pie in the Sky: The Hobo as American Cultural Hero in the Works of Jack London, John Dos Passos, and Jack Kerouac*. New York: Citadel, 1964. [C-170 Ctdl]

16 FIEDLER, Leslie. "Adolescence and Maturity in the American Novel." *An End to Innocence: Essays on Culture and Politics*. Boston: Beacon Press, 1955, 191–210. [BP4-Bea]

17 FIEDLER, Leslie A. "The Breakthrough: The American-Jewish Novelist and the Fictional Image of the Jew." *Midstream*, IV (1958), 15–35. Also in 14.10.

18 FIEDLER, Leslie. *The Jew in the American Novel*. Herzl Institute Pamphlet No. 10. New York: Herzl Press, 1959.

19 FIEDLER, Leslie. "The Novel and America." *PR*, XXVII (1956), 41–61.

20 FONZI, Bruno. "The American Novel and Italian Fiction." *Confluence*, II (1953), 23–30.

1   FREDERICK, John T. "Fiction of the Second World War." *CE*, XVII (1956), 197–204; *EJ*, XLIV (1955), 451–458.

2   FREY, John R. "Postwar German Reactions to American Literature." *JEGP*, LIV (1955), 173–194.

3   FREEDMAN, William. "American Jewish Fiction: So What's the Big Deal?" *ChiR*, XIX, i (1966), 90–107.

4   FROHOCK, W. M. *The Novel of Violence in America*. Rev. and enlarged ed. Dallas, Texas: Southern Methodist Univ. Press, 1957. [BP176-Bea]

5   GALLOWAY, David. *The Absurd Hero in American Fiction*. Austin, Tex.: Univ. of Texas Press, 1966. [Updike, Styron, Bellow, Salinger; including useful checklists of these novelists.]

6   GELFANT, Blanche Housman. *The American City Novel*. Norman, Okla.: Univ. of Oklahoma Press, 1954. [Anderson, Wolfe, Dos Passos, Farrell, Algren.]

7   GLICKSBERG, Charles I. "Negro Fiction in America." *SAQ*, XLV (1946), 477–488.

8   GLOSTER, Hugh Morris. *Negro Voices in American Fiction*. Chapel Hill, N.C.: Univ. of North Carolina Press, 1948.

9   GOLD, Herbert. "The Mystery of Personality in the Novel." *PR*, XXIV (1957), 453–462.

10 GOLD, Herbert. "Truth and Falsity in the Novel." *HudR*, VIII (1955), 410–422.

11 GUTTMANN, Allen. "The Conversion of the Jews." *WSCL*, VI (1965), 161–176. [The modern Jewish novel in America.]

12 GUTTMANN, Allen. "Jewish Radicals, Jewish Writers." *ASch*, XXXII (1963), 563–575.

13 HACKETT, Alice P. *Seventy Years of Best Sellers, 1895–1965*. New York: Bowker, 1967.

14 HARPER, Howard M., Jr. *Desperate Faith: A Study of Bellow, Salinger, Mailer, Baldwin, and Updike*. Chapel Hill, N.C.: Univ. of North Carolina Press, 1967.

15 HART, James D. "Platitudes of Piety: Religion and the Popular Modern Novel." *AQ*, VI (1954), 311–322.

16 HART, James D. *The Popular Book: A History of America's Literary Taste*. New York: Oxford Univ. Press, 1950. [Ca149-Calif]

17 HASSAN, Ihab H. "The Novel of Outrage: A Minority Voice in Postwar American Fiction." *ASch*, XXXIV (1965), 239–253.

18 HASSAN, Ihab H. *Radical Innocence: Studies in the Contemporary American Novel*. Princeton, N.J.: Princeton Univ. Press, 1961. [CN/85-CN]

19 HASSAN, Ihab H. "The Victim: Images of Evil in Recent American Fiction." *CE*, XXI (1959), 140–146. [Bowles, Mailer, Salinger, Purdy, McCullers.]

20 HERSEY, John. "The Novel of Contemporary History." *Atlantic*, CLXXXIV (1949), 80–84.

1 HICKS, Granville. "Fiction and Social Criticism." *CE*, XIII (1952), 355–361; *EJ*, XLI (1952), 173–179.

2 HILL, Herbert, ed. *Anger and Beyond: The Negro Writer in the United States.* New York: Harper & Row, 1966.

3 HOFFMAN, Frederick J. "Dogmatic Innocence: Self-Assertion in Modern American Literature." *TQ*, VI, ii (1963), 152–161.

4 HOFFMAN, Frederick J. *Freudianism and the Literary Mind.* Baton Rouge, La.: Lousiana State Univ. Press, 1957. [L-17-LSU]

5 HOFFMAN, Frederick J. "The Sense of Place." See 14.3. [Welty, Roberts, Faulkner, and other southern writers.]

6 HOLMAN, C. Hugh. *Three Modes of Modern Southern Fiction: Ellen Glasgow, William Faulkner, Thomas Wolfe.* Athens, Ga.: Univ. of Georgia Press, 1966. [Stresses regional differentiation.]

7 HOLMES, John C. "Existentialism and the Novel: Notes and Questions." *ChiR*, XIII (1959), 144–151. [Hemingway, Algren, Kerouac.]

8 HOWE, Irving. "Mass Society and Post-Modern Fiction." *PR*, XXVI (1959), 420–436. Also in 4.1 and 14.10.

9 HUGHES, Carl M. *The Negro Novelist.* New York: Citadel, 1953.

10 HUGHES, D. J. "Character in Contemporary Fiction." *MR*, III (1962), 788–795.

11 HYMAN, Stanley Edgar. "The Negro Writer in America: An Exchange. I. The Folk Tradition." *PR*, XXV (1958) 197–211.

12 KAROLIDES, Nicholas J. *The Pioneer in the American Novel, 1900–1950.* Norman, Okla.: Univ. of Oklahoma Press, 1967.

13 Kazin, Alfred. "American Naturalism: Reflections from Another Era." *NMQ*, XX (1950), 50–60.

14 KNOX, George. "The Negro Novelist's Sensibility and the Outsider Theme." *WHR*, XI (1957), 137–148.

15 KOHLER, Dayton. "Time in the Modern Novel." *EJ*, XXXVII (1948), 331–340; *CE*, X (1948), 15–24.

16 KRAUSE, Sydney J., ed. *Essays on Determinism in American Literature.* Kent, Ohio: Kent State Univ. Press, 1964.

17 LEHAN, Richard. "Camus' American Affinities." *Symposium*, XIII (1959), 255–270. [Hemingway, Faulkner, Bellow, Bowles.]

18 LEHAN, Richard. "Existentialism in Recent American Fiction: The Demonic Quest." *TSLL*, I (1959), 181–202. Also in 14.10. [Bowles, Bellow, Ellison, Wright.]

19 LESSER, Simon O. *Fiction and the Unconscious.* Boston: Beacon Press, 1957. [V-97-Vin]

20 LEVIN, Harry. "Some European Views of Contemporary American Literature." *AQ*, I (1949), 264–279.

21 LYONS, John O. *The College Novel in America.* Carbondale, Ill.: Southern Illinois Univ. Press, 1962.

1 MACLEAN, Hugh. "Conservatism in Modern American Fiction." *CE,* XV (1954), 315–325. [Fitzgerald, Faulkner, Marquand.]

2 MALIN, Irving. *Jews and Americans.* Carbondale, Ill.: Southern Illinois Univ. Press, 1965. [Bellow, Roth, Malamud.]

3 MALIN, Irving. *New American Gothic.* Carbondale, Ill.: Southern Illinois Univ. Press, 1962. [Capote, Purdy, O'Connor, Hawkes, McCuller, Salinger.]

4 MARCUS, Steven. "The American Negro in Search of Identity." *Commentary,* XVI (1953), 456–463. [Review-article on Ellison, Wright, Baldwin.]

5 MAXWELL, D. E. S. "Modern American Fiction and Its Inheritance." *American Fiction: The Intellectual Background.* New York: Columbia Univ. Press, 1963, 265–287.

6 MC COLE, C. John. *Lucifer at Large.* New York: Longmans, 1937.

7 MENCKEN, H. L. "The American Novel." See 14.15.

8 MEYER, Roy W. *The Middle Western Farm Novel in the Twentieth Century.* Lincoln, Nebr.: Univ. of Nebraska Press, 1965.

9 MILLGATE, Michael. *American Social Fiction: James to Cozzens.* New York: Barnes & Noble, 1964 (Orig.). [430–B&N]

10 MILNE, Gordon. *The American Political Novel.* Norman, Okla.: Univ. of Oklahoma Press, 1966.

11 MITCHELL, Stephen O. "Alien Vision: The Techniques of Science Fiction." *MFS,* IV (1958), 346–356.

12 MIZENER, Arthur. "The Novel of Manners in America." *KR,* XII (1950), 1–19.

13 MIZENER, Arthur. "The Thin Intelligent Face of American Fiction." *KR,* XVII (1955), 507–524.

14 MOTT, Frank Luther. *Golden Multitudes: The Story of Best Sellers in the United States.* New York: Macmillan, 1947.

15 MUELLER, Gustav E. "Philosophy in the Twentieth Century American Novel." *JAAC,* XVI (1958), 471–481.

16 MULLER, Herbert J. "Impressionism in Fiction." *ASch,* VII (1938), 355–367.

17 O'CONNOR, William Van. "The Novel of Experience." *Crit,* I (1956), 37–44.

18 RAHV, Philip. "Proletarian Literature." *SoR,* IV (1939), 616–628.

19 RIDEOUT, Walter B. *The Radical Novel in the United States: 1900–1954.* Cambridge, Mass.: Harvard Univ. Press, 1956. [AC 81-Am Cen]

20 ROTH, Philip. "Writing American Fiction." *Commentary,* XXXI (1961), 222–233.

21 SARTRE, Jean-Paul. "American Novelists in French Eyes. *Atlantic,* CLVIII (Aug., 1946), 114–118.

22 SCHOLES, Robert E. "The Modern American Novel and the Mason-Dixon Line." *GaR,* XIV (1960), 193–204.

1 SCHWARTZ, Delmore. "The Duchess' Red Shoes." *PR*, XX (1953), 55–73. [Takes issue with Trilling and Aldridge on the contemporary novel of manners.]

2 SMITH, Hugh L., Jr. "Jazz in the American Novel." *EJ*, XLVII (1958), 467–478.

3 SMITH, Thelma M. and Ward L. MINER. *Transatlantic Migration: The Contemporary American Novel in France.* Durham, N.C.: Duke Univ. Press, 1955.

4 STAFFORD, Jean. "The Psychological Novel." *KR*, X (1948), 214–227.

5 STRAUSS, Harold. "Realism in the Proletarian Novel." *YR*, XXVIII (1938), 360–374.

6 STUCKEY, W. J. *The Pulitzer Prize Novels: A Critical Look Backward.* Norman, Okla.: Univ. of Oklahoma Press, 1966.

7 SUTHERLAND, Donald. "Time on Our Hands." *YFS*, No. 10 (1953), 5–13. [Time in the modern French novel, with references to Faulkner, Dos Passos, et al.]

8 THORP, Margaret. "The Motion Picture and the Novel." *AQ*, III (1951), 195–203.

9 WALCUTT, Charles Child. *American Literary Naturalism: A Divided Stream.* Minneapolis, Minn.: Univ. of Minnesota Press, 1956.

10 WALCUTT, Charles Child. "Fear Motifs in the Literature Between Two Wars." *SAQ*, XLVI (1947), 227–238.

11 WALCUTT, Charles Child. "The Regional Novel and Its Future." *ArQ*, I (1945), 17–27.

12 WALDMEIR, Joseph J. "Novelists of Two Wars." *Nation*, CLXXXVII (Nov. 1, 1958), 304–307.

13 WEST, Robert H. "Science Fiction and Its Ideas." *GaR*, XV (1961), 276–286.

Collections of Studies of the American Novel

14 ALDRIDGE, John W., ed. *Critiques and Essays on Modern Fiction, 1920–1951.* New York: Ronald, 1952.

15 ALDRIDGE, John W. *In Search of Heresy.* New York: McGraw-Hill, 1956.

16 AUCHINCLOSS, Louis. *Pioneers & Caretakers: A Study of Nine American Women Novelists.* Minneapolis, Minn.: Univ. of Minnesota Press, 1965. [Includes essays on Roberts, Porter, Stafford, McCarthy, McCullers.] [6916-Delta-Dell]

17 BALAKIAN, Nona and Charles SIMMONS, eds. *The Creative Present: Notes on Contemporary American Fiction.* New York: Doubleday, 1963. [Essays by various hands.]

1 BODE, Carl, ed. *The Young Rebel in American Literature: Seven Lectures.* London: William Heinemann, 1959. [Includes lectures, by American scholars and critics for an English audience, on Lewis, Fitzgerald, Steinbeck, and Faulkner.]

2 COWLEY, Malcolm, ed. *After the Genteel Tradition: American Writers, 1910–1930.* Rev. ed. Carbondale, Ill.: Southern Illinois Univ. Press, 1964. [Reissue of a collection of essays published in 1937.]

3 COWLEY, Malcolm, ed. *Writers at Work: The "Paris Review" Interviews.* New York: Viking, 1958. [C52-Comp]

4 GARDINER, Harold C., S.J., ed. *Fifty Years of the American Novel: A Christian Appraisal.* New York: Scribner, 1951. [Essays by various hands.]

5 GEISMAR, Maxwell. *American Moderns: A Mid-Century View of Contemporary Fiction.* New York: Hill & Wang, 1958. [Includes essays on Bellow, Salinger, Jones, Styron.] [AC44-Am Cen]

6 GREEN, Martin. *Re-Appraisals: Some Commonsense Readings in American Literature.* London: Hugh Evelyn, 1963. [An iconoclastic survey; includes chapters on Faulkner, Salinger, Nabokov.] [N400-Nort]

7 HICKS, Granville. *The Living Novel: A Symposium.* New York: Macmillan, 1957. [Contributions by Bellow, Ellison, Morris, and others.] [05192-Collr]

8 KOSTELANETZ, Richard, ed. *On Contemporary Literature.* New York: Avon, 1965. [CS-2-Avon]

9 LITZ, A. Walton. *Modern American Fiction: Essays in Criticism.* New York: Oxford Univ. Press, 1963. [GB100]

10 MALIN, Irving, ed. *Psychoanalysis and American Fiction.* New York: Dutton, 1965. [Essays by various hands, including studies of Cather, Faulkner, Caldwell, Bellow.] [D-162-Duttn]

11 MIZENER, Arthur. *The Sense of Life in the Modern Novel.* Boston: Houghton Mifflin, 1964 (Orig.). [Includes essays on Cozzens, Faulkner, Fitzgerald, Hemingway, Salinger, Updike.] [HM]

12 MOORE, Harry T., ed. *Contemporary American Novelists.* Carbondale, Ill.: Southern Illinois Univ. Press, 1964. [AB-23-SIU]

13 MORGAN, H. Wayne. *Writers in Transition: Seven Americans.* New York: Hill & Wang, 1963. [Cather, Anderson, and Wolfe] [AC58-Am Cen]

14 MORRIS, Wright. *The Territory Ahead.* New York: Harcourt, Brace, 1958. [Includes essays on Hemingway, Fitzgerald, Faulkner, Wolfe.] [37-Athen]

15 O'CONNOR, William Van, ed. *Forms of Modern Fiction: Essays Collected in Honor of Joseph Warren Beach.* Minneapolis, Minn.: Univ. of Minnesota Press, 1948. [Includes essays on Fitzgerald, Hemingway, Faulkner, Warren.] [MB16-Ind]

16 PLIMPTON, George, ed. *Writers at Work: The "Paris Review" Interviews.* Second Series. Introd. by Van Wyck Brooks. New York: Viking, 1963. [Interviews with Miller, Porter, Hemingway, McCarthy, Ellison.]

1 PODHORETZ, Norman. *Doings and Undoings: The Fifties and After in American Writing.* New York: Farrar, Straus, 1964. [Includes essays on Faulkner, Fitzgerald, West, O'Hara, McCarthy, Mailer, Bellow, Baldwin, Updike.] [N260-Noon]

2 RUBIN, Louis D., Jr. and John Rees MOORE, eds. *The Idea of an American Novel.* New York: Crowell-Collier, 1961. [The American novel in general, with individual pieces on Lewis, Hemingway, Fitzgerald, Farrell, Wolfe, Faulkner, and Warren.]

3 RUBIN, Louis D., Jr. and Robert D. JACOBS. *South: Modern Southern Literature in its Cultural Setting.* Garden City, N.Y.: Doubleday, 1961.

4 RUBIN, Louis D., Jr. and Robert D. JACOBS. *Southern Renascence: The Literature of the Modern South.* Baltimore, Md.: Johns Hopkins Press, 1953. [JH-13-JHP]

5 SHAPIRO, Charles, ed. *Twelve Original Essays on Great American Novels.* Detroit, Mich.: Wayne State Univ. Press, 1958. [Anderson, Fitzgerald, Hemingway, Faulkner.] [WB13-Wayne]

6 STALLMAN, Robert W. *The Houses that James Built and Other Literary Studies.* East Lansing, Mich.: Michigan State Univ. Press, 1961. [Includes essays on Fitzgerald, Hemingway, Faulkner.]

7 STEGNER, Wallace, ed. *The American Novel from James Fenimore Cooper to William Faulkner.* New York: Basic Books, 1965. [Includes essays on Anderson, Lewis, Fitzgerald, Hemingway, Wolfe, Faulkner.]

8 SUTHERLAND, William O. S., ed. *Six Contemporary Novels: Six Introductory Essays in Modern Fiction.* Austin, Tex.: Univ. of Texas Dept. of English, 1962.

9 VAN GELDER, Robert. *Writers and Writing.* New York: Scribner, 1946. [Brief interviews reprinted from the *New York Times Book Review*.]

10 WALDMEIR, Joseph J., ed. *Recent American Fiction: Some Critical Views* Boston: Houghton Mifflin, 1963 (Orig.). [HM]

11 WESTBROOK, Max, ed. *The Modern American Novel: Essays in Criticism.* New York: Random House, 1966. [SLL-6-RH]

12 WHIPPLE, T. K. *Spokesmen: Modern Writers and American Life.* New York: Appleton, 1928. [Includes essays on Anderson, Cather, Lewis.] [Cal-82 Calif]

13 WHIPPLE, T. K. *Study Out the Land.* Berkeley and Los Angeles, Calif.: Univ. of California Press, 1943. [Includes essays on Steinbeck and Dos Passos.]

14 WILSON, Edmund. *The Shores of Light: A Literary Chronicle of the Twenties and Thirties.* New York: Farrar, Straus & Young, 1952. [V181-Vin]

15 ZABEL, Morton Dauwen, ed. *Literary Opinion in America.* Rev. ed. New York: Harper, 1951. 2 vols. [TB/3013 Torch; TB/3014 Torch]

Contemporary American Novelists

Aiken, Conrad (1889–)

TEXTS

1 *Collected Novels.* Introd. by R. P. Blackmur. New York: Holt, Rinehart, & Winston, 1964.

2 *Ushant: An Essay.* New York: Duell, Sloan, & Pearce, 1952. [Autobiographical.]

BIOGRAPHICAL AND CRITICAL BOOKS

3 DENNEY, Reuel. *Conrad Aiken.* UMPAW, No. 38. Minneapolis, Minn.: Univ. of Minnesota Press, 1964. [UMP]

4 HOFFMAN, Frederick J. *Conrad Aiken.* New York: Twayne, 1962. [T-17-C&UPS]

5 MARTIN, Jay. *Conrad Aiken: A Life of His Art.* Princeton, N.J.: Princeton Univ. Press, 1962.

BIOGRAPHICAL AND CRITICAL ESSAYS

6 ALDRICH, Jennifer. "The Deciphered Heart: Conrad Aiken's Poetry and Prose Fiction." *SR,* LXXV (1967), 485–520.

7 BROWN, Ashley. "An Interview with Conrad Aiken." *Shenandoah,* XV, i (1963), 18–40.

8 SCHORER, Mark. "The Life in Fiction." *Wake,* XI (1952), 57–60.

Algren, Nelson (1909–)

TEXTS

9 *Notes from a Sea Diary: Hemingway All the Way.* New York: Putnam, 1965. [Essays written in the spirit of Hemingway.] [R-973-Crest]

10 DONOHUE, H. E. F. *Conversations with Nelson Algren.* New York: Hill & Wang, 1964. [S1134-Berk]

BIOGRAPHICAL AND CRITICAL ESSAYS

11 ANDERSON, Alston and Terry SOUTHERN. "Nelson Algren." See 13.3. [*A Paris Review* Interview.]

1 BLUESTONE, George. "Nelson Algren." *WR*, XXII (1957), 27–44.

2 GEISMAR, Maxwell. "Nelson Algren: The Iron Sanctuary." *CE*, XIV (1953), 311–315; *EJ*, XLII (1953), 121–125.

3 LIPTON, Lawrence. "A Voyeur's View of the Wild Side: Nelson Algren and His Critics." *ChiR*, X (1957), 4–14.

4 PERLONGO, Robert A. "Interview with Nelson Algren." *ChiR*, XI (1957), 92–98.

Anderson, Sherwood (1876–1941)

TEXTS

5 *The Modern Writer*. San Francisco, Calif.: Lantern Press, 1925.

6 *Sherwood Anderson's Memoirs*. New York: Harcourt, Brace, 1942.

7 *Sherwood Anderson's Notebook*. New York: Boni & Liveright, 1926.

8 *A Story-Teller's Story*. New York: B. W. Huebsch, 1924. [Evergreen-E109]

9 *Tar: A Midwest Childhood*. New York: Boni & Liveright, 1926.

10 *Windy McPherson's Son*. Introd. by Wright Morris. Chicago, Ill.: Univ. of Chicago Press, 1965. [P250-Phoen]

11 *Winesburg, Ohio*. Introd. by Malcolm Cowley. New York: Viking, 1960. [C39-Comp]

12 *A Writer's Concept of Realism*. An Address delivered on Jan. 20, 1939, at Olivet College. Olivet, Mich.: Olivet College, 1939. [A pamphlet.]

13 *Letters of Sherwood Anderson*. Ed. by Howard Mumford Jones and Walter B. Rideout. Boston: Little, Brown, 1953.

14 *The Portable Sherwood Anderson*. Ed., with introd., by Horace Gregory. New York: Viking, 1949. [P42-Vik]

15 *The Sherwood Anderson Reader*. Ed., with introd., by Paul Rosenfeld. Boston: Houghton Mifflin, 1947.

BIBLIOGRAPHY

16 SHEEHY, Eugene P. and Kenneth A. LOHF. *Sherwood Anderson: A Bibliography*. Los Gatos, Calif.: Talisman Press, 1960.

BIOGRAPHICAL AND CRITICAL BOOKS

17 ANDERSON, David D. *Sherwood Anderson: An Introduction and Interpretation*. New York: Holt, Rinehart & Winston, 1967.

1   BURBANK, Rex. *Sherwood Anderson.* New York: Twayne, 1964. [T-65-C&UPS]

2   CHASE, Cleveland B. *Sherwood Anderson.* New York: R. M. McBride, 1927. [A brief survey in the Modern American Writers series.]

3   DERLETH, August. *Three Literary Men: A Memoir of Sinclair Lewis, Sherwood Anderson, Edgar Lee Masters.* New York: Candlelight Press, 1963.

4   FAGIN, N. Bryllion. *The Phenomenon of Sherwood Anderson: A Study in American Life and Letters.* Baltimore, Md.: Rossi-Bryn, 1927.

5   HOWE, Irving. *Sherwood Anderson.* New York: Sloane, 1951. [SP-34-Stan U]

6   SCHEVILL, James. *Sherwood Anderson: His Life and Work.* Denver, Colo.: Univ. of Denver Press, 1951.

7   WEBER, Brom. *Sherwood Anderson.* UMPAW, No. 43. Minneapolis, Minn.: Univ. of Minnesota Press, 1964. [UMP]

8   WHITE, Ray L., ed. *The Achievement of Sherwood Anderson: Essays in Criticism.* Chapel Hill, N.C.: Univ. of North Carolina Press, 1966. [Essays by various hands.]

BIOGRAPHICAL AND CRITICAL ESSAYS

9   ANDERSON, Sherwood. "Man and His Imagination." *The Intent of the Artist.* Ed. by Augusto Centeno. Princeton, N.J.: Princeton Univ. Press, 1941.

10   BUDD, Louis J. "The Grotesques of Anderson and Wolfe." *MFS,* V (1959) 304–310.

11   CALVERTON, V. F. "Sherwood Anderson: A Study in Sociological Criticism." *ModQ,* II, ii (1924), 82–118.

12   CARGILL, Oscar. See 2.7.

13   CRANE, Hart. "Sherwood Anderson." *DD,* II (1921), 42–45.

14   DELL, Floyd. "On Being Sherwood Anderson's Literary Father." *NLB,* V (1961), 315–321.

15   FARRELL, James T. "A Memoir of Sherwood Anderson." *Perspective,* VII (1954), 83–88.

16   FAULKNER, William. "Prophets of the New Age: Sherwood Anderson." *Dallas Morning News,* April 26, 1925, Sec. III, p. 7. Repr. in *PULC,* XVIII (1957), 89–94.

17   FAULKNER, William. "Sherwood Anderson: An Appreciation." *Atlantic,* CXCI (June, 1953), 27–29. Also in 17.8.

18   FEIBLEMAN, James K. "Memories of Sherwood Anderson." *Shenandoah,* XIII (1962), 32–45.

19   FRANK, Waldo. "Emerging Greatness." *SeA,* I (1916), 73–78. Also in 17.8.

20   FRANK, Waldo. "*Winesburg, Ohio* after Twenty Years." *Story,* XXIX (Sept.–Oct., 1941), 29–33. Also in 17.8.

21   FRIEND, Julius. "The Philosophy of Sherwood Anderson." *Story,* XXIX (Sept.–Oct., 1941), 37–41.

1 FUSSELL, Edwin. *"Winesburg, Ohio:* Art and Isolation." *MFS, VI* (1960), 106–114. Also in 17.8.

2 GEISMAR, Maxwell. "Sherwood Anderson: Last of the Townsmen." See 5.17.

3 GELFANT, Blanche. "A Novel of Becoming." See 9.6. [Anderson as urban novelist.]

4 GOLD, Herbert. *"Winesburg, Ohio:* The Purity and Cunning of Sherwood Anderson." *HudR,* X (1958), 548–557. Also in 13.9 and 14.5.

5 HANSEN, Harry. "Anderson in Chicago." *Story,* XXIX (Sept.–Oct., 1941), 34–36.

6 HANSEN, Harry. "Sherwood Anderson, Corn-Fed Mystic, Historian of the Middle Age of Man." *Midwest Portraits: A Book of Memories and Friendships.* New York: Harcourt Brace, 1923, 109–179.

7 HARTWICK, Harry. "Broken Face Gargoyles." See 6.3. [On Anderson's "grotesques."]

8 HATCHER, Harlan. "Freudian Psychology and the Sex Age." See 6.5.

9 HERBST, Josephine. "Ubiquitous Critics and the Author." *NLB,* V (1958), 1–13.

10 HOFFMAN, Frederick J. "Anderson—Psychoanalyst by Default." See 10.4.

11 HOFFMAN, Frederick J. "The Voices of Sherwood Anderson." *Shenandoah,* XIII (1962), 5–19. Also in 17.8.

12 HOWE, Irving. "Sherwood Anderson: An American as Artist." *KR,* XIII (1951), 193–203.

13 JOSEPH, Gerhard. "The American Triumph of the Egg: Anderson's 'The Egg' and Fitzgerald's *The Great Gatsby.*" *Criticism,* VII (1965), 131–140.

14 KAZIN, Alfred. "The New Realism: Sherwood Anderson and Sinclair Lewis." See 2.12 and 65.11.

15 LAWRY, Jon S. "The Artist in America: The Case of Sherwood Anderson." *BSUF,* VII, ii (1966), 15–26.

16 LOVETT, Robert Morss. "Sherwood Anderson, American." *VQR,* XVII (1941), 379–388. Also in 14.15.

17 MAHONEY, John J. "An Analysis of *Winesburg, Ohio.*" *JAAC,* XV (1956), 245–252.

18 PEARSON, Norman Holmes. "Anderson and the New Puritanism." *NLB,* II (Dec., 1948), 52–63.

19 PHILLIPS, William L. "The First Printing of Sherwood Anderson's *Winesburg, Ohio.*" *SB,* IV (1951), 211–213.

20 PHILLIPS, William L. "How Sherwood Anderson Wrote *Winesburg, Ohio.*" *AL,* XXIII (1951), 7–30. Also in 17.8.

21 RIDEOUT, Walter B. "The Simplicity of *Winesburg, Ohio.*" *Shenandoah,* XIII (1962), 13–21.

22 ROSENFELD, Paul. "Sherwood Anderson." *Dial,* LXXII (1922), 29–42. Repr. in Rosenfeld, *Port of New York.* New York: Harcourt, Brace, 1924, 175–198.

1 ROSENFELD, Paul. "Sherwood Anderson's Work." *Anglica* (Florence), I (1946), 66–88. Repr. as introd. to *The Sherwood Anderson Reader*. Boston: Houghton Mifflin, 1947.

2 SAN JUAN, Epifanio, Jr. "Vision and Reality: A Reconsideration of Sherwood Anderson's *Winesburg, Ohio*." *AL*, XXXV (1963), 137–155.

3 SULLIVAN, John H. "Winesburg Revisited." *AR*, XX (1960), 213–221.

4 THURSTON, Jarvis. "Anderson and *Winesburg:* Mysticism and Craft." *Accent*, XVI (1956), 107–128.

5 TRILLING, Lionel. "Sherwood Anderson." *KR*, III (1941), 293–302. Repr., with revisions, in *The Liberal Imagination*. New York: Viking, 1950, 20–31. Also in 12.14 and 17.8. [A13-Anch]

6 VAN DOREN, Carl. "Sinclair Lewis and Sherwood Anderson: A Study of Two Moralists." *Century*, CX (1925), 362–369.

7 WALCUTT, Charles Child. "Sherwood Anderson: Impressionism and the Buried Life." *SR*, LX (1952), 28–47. Also in 12.9 and 17.8.

8 WEBER, Brom. "Anderson and 'The Essence of Things'." *SR*, LIX (1951), 678–692.

9 WINTHER, S. K. "The Aura of Loneliness in Sherwood Anderson." *MFS*, V (1959), 145–152.

Baldwin, James (1924–   )

BIBLIOGRAPHY

10 FISCHER, Russell G. "James Baldwin: A Bibliography, 1947–1962." *BB*, XXIV (1965), 127–130.

11 KINDT, Kathleen A. "James Baldwin: A Checklist: 1947–1962." *BB*, XXIV (1965), 123–126.

BIOGRAPHICAL AND CRITICAL BOOKS

12 ECKMAN, Fern Marja. *The Furious Passage of James Baldwin*. New York: Evans, 1966. [Biographical.]

BIOGRAPHICAL AND CRITICAL ESSAYS

13 BONE, Robert A. "The Novels of James Baldwin." *TriQ*, No. 2 (1965), 3–20.

14 BOYLE, Kay. "Introducing James Baldwin." See 13.12.

15 BREIT, Harvey. "James Baldwin and Two Footnotes." See 12.17.

16 CHARNEY, Maurice. "James Baldwin's Quarrel with Richard Wright." *AQ*, XV (1963), 65–75.

17 COLES, Robert. "Baldwin's Burden." *PR*, XXXI (1964), 409–416.

1 GROSS, Theodore. "The World of James Baldwin." *Crit*, VII, ii (1965), 139–149.

2 JACOBSON, Dan. "James Baldwin as Spokesman." *Commentary*, XXXII (1961), 497–502.

3 KAZIN, Alfred. "The Essays of James Baldwin." *Contemporaries*. Boston: Little, Brown, 1962, 254–258.

4 KLEIN, Marcus. "James Baldwin: A Question of Identity." See 6.14.

5 MAC INNES, Colin. "Dark Angel: The Writings of James Baldwin." *Encounter*, XXI (1963), 22–33.

6 MARCUS, Steven. See 11.4.

7 NEWMAN, Charles. "The Lesson of the Master: Henry James and James Baldwin." *YR*, LVI (1966), 45–59.

8 PODHORETZ, Norman. "In Defense of James Baldwin." See 14.1. [On *Another Country*.]

9 SAYRE, Robert F. "James Baldwin's Other Country." See 13.12.

10 SPENDER, Stephen. "James Baldwin: Voice of a Revolution." *PR*, XXX (1963), 256–260.

11 STANDLEY, Fred L. "James Baldwin: The Crucial Situation." *SAQ*, LXV (1966), 371–381.

12 WATSON, Edward A. "The Novels of James Baldwin: Casebook of a 'Lover's War' with the United States." *MR*, VI (1965), 385–402.

Barth, John (1930–   )

BIBLIOGRAPHY

13 BRYER, Jackson R. "John Barth." *Crit.*, VI, ii (1963), 86–89.

BIOGRAPHICAL AND CRITICAL ESSAYS

14 KIELY, Benedict. "Ripeness Was Not All: John Barth's *Giles Goat-boy*." *HC*, III, v (1966), 1–12. [A review-article.]

15 MILLER, Russell H. "*The Sot-Weed Factor*: A Contemporary Mock-Epic." *Crit*, VIII, ii (1966), 88–100.

16 NOLAND, Richard W. "John Barth and the Novel of Comic Nihilism." *WSCL*, VII (1966), 239–257.

17 ROVIT, Earl. "The Novel as Parody: John Barth." *Crit*, VI, ii (1963), 77–85.

18 SCHICKEL, Richard. "The Floating Opera." *Crit*, VI, ii (1963), 53–67.

19 SMITH, Herbert F. "Barth's Endless Road." *Crit*, VI, ii (1963), 68–76.

20 STUBBS, John C. "John Barth as a Novelist of Ideas: The Themes of Value and Identity." *Crit*, VIII, ii (1966), 101–116.

1 TRACHTENBERG, Alan. "Barth and Hawkes: Two Fabulists." *Crit*, VI, ii, (1963), 4–18.

Bellow, Saul (1915–   )

BIBLIOGRAPHY

2 SCHNEIDER, Harold W. "Two Bibliographies: Saul Bellow, William Styron." *Crit*, III (1960), 71–91.

BIOGRAPHICAL AND CRITICAL BOOKS

3 MALIN, Irving, ed. *Saul Bellow and the Critics*. New York: New York Univ. Press, 1967 (Orig.). [Essays by various hands.] [NYU]

4 OPDAHL, Keith M. *The Novels of Saul Bellow: An Introduction*. University Park, Pa.: Penn State Univ. Press, 1967.

5 ROVIT, Earl. *Saul Bellow*. UMPAW, No. 65. Minneapolis, Minn.: Univ. of Minnesota Press, 1967. (UMP)

6 TANNER, Tony. *Saul Bellow*. Edinburgh: Oliver & Boyd, 1965.

BIOGRAPHICAL AND CRITICAL ESSAYS

7 ALDRIDGE, John W. "The Complacency of Herzog." See 5.2 and 21.3.

8 ALDRIDGE, John W. "The Society of Three Novels." See 12.15. [Includes discussion of *Augie March*.]

9 AXTHELM, Peter M. "The Full Perception: Bellow." *The Modern Confessional Novel*. New Haven, Conn.: Yale Univ. Press, 1967, 128–177.

10 BAKER, Sheridan. "Saul Bellow's Bout with Chivalry." *Criticism*, VIII (1966), 109–122.

11 BAUMBACH, Jonathan. "The Double Vision: *The Victim*." See 5.4.

12 BELLOW, Saul. "Deep Readers of the World, Beware!" *NYTBR*, Feb. 15, 1959, 1, 34. [A caveat to symbol-hunters.]

13 BELLOW, Saul. "Distractions of a Fiction Writer." *New World Writing* (12th Mentor Selection). New York: New American Library, 1957, 229–243. Also in 13.7.

14 BELLOW, Saul. "How I Wrote Augie March's Story." *NYTBR*, Jan. 31, 1954, 3, 17.

15 BERGLER, Edmund. "Writers of Half-Talent." *AI*, XIV (Summer, 1957), 155–164. [Evaluation of *Augie March* from a psychoanalytical point of view.]

16 BRADBURY, Malcolm. "Saul Bellow's *Herzog*." *CritQ*, VII (1965), 269–278.

17 BRADBURY, Malcolm. "Saul Bellow and the Naturalist Tradition." *REL*, IV, iv (1963), 80–92.

18 BRADBURY, Malcolm. "Saul Bellow's *The Victim*." *CritQ*, V (1963), 119–128.

19 CHASE, Richard. "The Adventures of Saul Bellow: The Progress of a Novelist." *Commentary*, XXVII (1959), 323–330. Also in 21.3.

Cabell, James Branch (1879–1958)

TEXTS

1 *The Works of James Branch Cabell.* Storisende Edition. 18 vols. New York: McBride, 1927–1930.

2 *As I Remember It: Some Epilogues in Recollection.* New York: McBride, 1955. [Autobiographical.]

3 *Quiet, Please.* Gainesville, Fla.: Univ. of Florida Press, 1952. [Autobiographical.]

BIBLIOGRAPHY

4 BREWER, Frances Joan. *James Branch Cabell: A Bibliography of His Writings, Biography and Criticism.* Foreword by James Branch Cabell. Charlottesville, Va.: Univ. of Virginia Press, 1957. [Vol. I of two.]

5 BRUCCOLI, Matthew J. *James Branch Cabell, a Bibliography, Part II: Notes on the Cabell Collections of the University of Virginia.* Charlottesville, Va.: Univ. of Virginia Press, 1957.

BIOGRAPHICAL AND CRITICAL BOOKS

6 COLUM, Padraic and Margaret Freeman CABELL, eds. *Between Friends: Letters of James Branch Cabell and Others.* Introd. by Carl Van Vechten. New York: Harcourt, Brace & World, 1962.

7 DAVIS, Joe Lee. *James Branch Cabell.* New York: Twayne, 1962. [T-21-C&UPS]

8 MC NEILL, Warren A. *Cabellian Harmonics.* With an introd. note by James Branch Cabell. New York: Random House, 1928. [Cabell's uses of music and poetry.]

9 MENCKEN, H. L. *James Branch Cabell.* New York: McBride, 1927.

10 TARRANT, Desmond. *James Branch Cabell: The Dream and the Reality.* Norman, Okla.: Univ. of Oklahoma Press, 1967.

11 VAN DOREN, Carl. *James Branch Cabell.* Rev. ed. New York: The Literary Guild, 1932.

12 WELLS, Arvin R. *Jesting Moses: A Study in Cabellian Comedy.* Gainesville, Fla.: Univ. of Florida Press, 1962.

BIOGRAPHICAL AND CRITICAL ESSAYS

13 ALLEN, Gay Wilson. "Jurgen and Faust." *SR*, XXXIX (1931), 485–492.

14 BEACH, Joseph Warren. "Mr. Cabell." *The Outlook for American Prose.* Chicago: Univ. of Chicago Press, 1926, 63–80.

1 BOYNTON, Percy. "Mr. Cabell Expounds Himself." *EJ*, XII (1923), 258–265.

2 CABELL, James Branch. "Recipes for Writers." *Colophon*, pt. 7 (1931), 1–8.

3 CABELL, James Branch. "They Buried Me Alive." *AMer*, LXXIII (1951), 96–105.

4 CARGILL, Oscar. See 2.7. [Adverse critique.]

5 EDGAR, Pelham. "Two Anti-Realists: Willa Cather and Cabell." *The Art of the Novel*. New York: Macmillan, 1933, 255–267.

6 FISHWICK, Marshall W. "Cabell and Glasgow: Tradition in Search of Meaning." *Shenandoah*, VIII (1957), 24–35.

7 GLASGOW, Ellen. *The Woman Within*. New York: Harcourt, Brace, 1954, 129–136. [Memoir of Miss Glasgow's friendship with Cabell.]

8 HARTWICK, Harry. "The Journeys of Jurgen." See 6.3.

9 HATCHER, Harlan. "James Branch Cabell." See 6.5.

10 HERGESHEIMER, Joseph. "James Branch Cabell." *AMer*, XIII (1928), 38–47.

11 HIMELICK, Raymond. "Cabell and the Modern Temper." *SAQ*, LVIII (1959), 176–184.

12 HIMELICK, Raymond. "Cabell, Shelley, and the 'Incorrigible Flesh'." *SAQ*, XLVII (1948), 88–95.

13 HIMELICK, Raymond. "Figures of Cabell." *MFS*, II (1956), 214–220.

14 HOOKER, Edward N. "Something About Cabell." *SR*, XXXVII (1929), 192–203.

15 HOWARD, Leon. "Figures of Allegory." *SR*, XLII (1934), 54–66.

16 JACK, Peter Monro. "The James Branch Cabell Period." See 13.2.

17 MC INTYRE, C. F. "Mr. Cabell's Cosmos." *SR*, XXXVIII (1930), 278–285.

18 MICHAUD, Régis. "James Branch Cabell and the Escape to Poictesme," and "James Branch Cabell on the High Place." See 6.17.

19 PARKER, William R. "A Key to Cabell." *EJ*, XXI (1932), 431–440.

20 PARKS, Edd Winfield. "James Branch Cabell." See 14.4.

21 PARRINGTON, Vernon Louis. "The Incomparable Mr. Cabell." *Main Currents in American Thought*, Vol. III: *The Beginnings of Critical Realism in America*. New York: Harcourt, Brace, 1930, 335–345. [Cabell as "one of the great masters of English prose."] [H023-Hbgr]

22 RUBIN, Louis D., Jr. "A Southerner in Poictesme." *No Place on Earth: Ellen Glasgow, James Branch Cabell and Richmond-in-Virginia*. Austin, Tex.: Univ. of Texas Press, 1959, 50–80.

1 RUBIN, Louis D., Jr. "Two in Richmond: Ellen Glasgow and James Branch Cabell." *South: Modern Southern Literature and Its Cultural Setting*. Ed. by Louis D. Rubin, Jr. and Robert D. Jacobs. Garden City, N.Y.: Doubleday, 1961, 115–141.

2 TARRANT, Desmond. "James Branch Cabell (1879–1958): A Reappraisal." *Shenandoah*, IX (1958), 3–9.

3 VAN VECHTEN, Carl. "Mr. Cabell of Lichfield and Poictesme." *YULG*, XXIII (1948), 1–7.

4 WAGENKNECHT, Edward. "James Branch Cabell: The Anatomy of Romanticism." See 4.14.

5 WALPOLE, Hugh. "The Art of James Branch Cabell." *YR*, IX (1920), 684–698.

6 WILSON, Edmund. "The James Branch Cabell Case Reopened." *NY*, XXXII (April 21, 1956), 129–156. [Attempt to resuscitate Cabell's reputation.]

Caldwell, Erskine (1903–   )

BIOGRAPHICAL AND CRITICAL ESSAYS

7 BEACH, Joseph Warren. "Erskine Caldwell: The Comic Catharsis" and "Erskine Caldwell: Substitutes and Compensations." See 5.5.

8 BURKE, Kenneth. "Caldwell, Maker of Grotesques." *NR*, CXXXII (1935), 232–235. Repr. in Burke, *The Philosophy of Literary Form*. Baton Rouge, La.: Louisiana State Univ. Press, 1941. Also in 13.10.

9 CANTWELL, Robert. "Caldwell's Characters: Why Don't They Leave?" *GaR*, XI (1957), 252–264.

10 COLLINS, Carvel. "Erskine Caldwell at Work." *Atlantic*, CCII (July, 1958), 21–27.

11 FROHOCK, W. M. "Erskine Caldwell: Sentimental Gentleman from Georgia." *SWR*, XXXI (1946), 351–359.

12 HAZEL, Robert. "Notes on Erskine Caldwell." See 14.3.

13 KUBIE, L. S. " 'God's Little Acre!' An Analysis." *SatRL*, XI (1934), 305–306, 312.

14 MACLACHLAN, J. M. "Folk and Culture in the Novels of Erskine Caldwell." *SFQ*, IX (1945), 93–101.

15 VAN GELDER, Robert. "A Talk with Erskine Caldwell." See 14.9.

16 WADE, John D. "Sweet are the Uses of Degeneracy." *SoR*, I (1936), 449–466.

Capote, Truman (1924–   )

BIBLIOGRAPHY

1 WALL, Richard J. and Carl L. CRAYCRAFT. "A Checklist of Works About Truman Capote." *BNYPL*, LXXI (1967), 165–172.

BIOGRAPHICAL AND CRITICAL ESSAYS

2 ALDRIDGE, John W. "The World of Truman Capote." *WR*, XV (1951), 247–260.

3 CAPOTE, Truman. "The Art of Fiction." *ParisR*, No. 16 (1957), 35–51. Also in 13.3. [An interview.]

4 COLLINS, Carvel. "Other Voices." *ASch*, XXV (1955), 108–116.

5 HASSAN, Ihab H. "The Daydream and Nightmare of Narcissus." *WSCL*, I (1960), 5–21.

6 LEVINE, Paul. "Truman Capote: The Revelation of the Broken Image." *VQR*, XXXIV (1958), 600–617.

7 MENGELING, Marvin E. *"Other Voices, Other Rooms:* Oedipus Between the Covers." *AI*, XIX (1962), 361–374.

8 MORAVIA, Alberto. "Two American Writers (1949)." *SR*, LXVIII (1960), 473–481. [On Capote and Henry Miller.]

9 SCHORER, Mark. "McCullers and Capote: Basic Patterns." See 12.17.

Cather, Willa (1873–1947)

TEXTS

10 BENNETT, Mildred R., ed. *Early Stories of Willa Cather.* With notes. New York: Dodd, Mead, 1957.

11 CATHER, Willa. *On Writing.* New York: Knopf, 1949.

12 KATES, George N., ed. *Willa Cather in Europe: Her Own Story of the First Journey.* New York: Knopf, 1956.

13 SHIVELY, James R. *Writings from Willa Cather's Campus Years.* Lincoln, Nebr.: Univ. of Nebraska Press, 1950.

14 SLOTE, Bernice, ed. *The Kingdom of Art: Willa Cather's First Principles and Critical Statements, 1893–1896.* Selected and ed. with a commentary. Lincoln, Nebr.: Univ. of Nebraska Press, 1966.

15 TENNANT, Stephen, ed. *Willa Cather on Writing: Critical Studies on Writing as an Art.* New York: Knopf, 1953.

16 *Willa Cather's Collected Short Fiction, 1892–1912.* Introd. by Mildred R. Bennett. Lincoln, Nebr.: Univ. of Nebraska Press, 1965. [Includes useful bibliography of the short fiction.]

BIBLIOGRAPHY

1 ADAMS, Frederick B. "Willa Cather Early Years: Trial and Error." *Colophon*, I, no. 3 (1939).

2 ADAMS, Frederick B. "Willa Cather Middle Years: The Right Road Taken." *Colophon*, I, no. 4 (1940).

3 BROWN, E. K. "Willa Cather: The Benjamin D. Hitz Collection." *NLB*, No. 5 (Dec., 1950), 158–160.

4 HUTCHINSON, Phyllis Martin. "The Writings of Willa Cather: A List of Works by and about Her." *BNYPL*, LX (1956), 267–288, 338–356, 378–400.

BIOGRAPHICAL AND CRITICAL BOOKS

5 BENNETT, Mildred R. *The World of Willa Cather*. Rev. ed. Lincoln, Nebr.: Univ. of Nebraska Press, 1961. [BB112-Bison]

6 BLOOM, Edward A. and Lillian D. *Willa Cather's Gift of Sympathy*. Carbondale, Ill.: Southern Illinois Univ. Press, 1962. [AB-6-SIU]

7 BROWN, E. K. and Leon EDEL. *Willa Cather: A Critical Biography*. New York: Knopf, 1953.

8 DAICHES, David. *Willa Cather: A Critical Introduction*. Ithaca, N.Y.: Cornell Univ. Press, 1951. [05016-Collr]

9 LEWIS, Edith. *Willa Cather Living: A Personal Record*. New York: Knopf, 1953. [Memoir by Willa Cather's companion.]

10 RANDALL, John H., III. *The Landscape and the Looking Glass: Willa Cather's Search for Value*. Boston: Houghton Mifflin, 1960.

11 RAPIN, René. *Willa Cather*. New York: McBride, 1930. [Brief survey in the Modern American Writers series.]

12 SCHROETER, James, ed. *Willa Cather and Her Critics*. Ithaca, N.Y.: Cornell Univ. Press, 1967. [A selection of reviews, critical essays, and reminiscences, ranging from 1916 to the present.]

13 SERGEANT, Elizabeth Shepley. *Willa Cather: A Memoir*. Philadelphia: Lippincott, 1953.

14 VAN GHENT, Dorothy. *Willa Cather*. UMPAW, No. 36. Minneapolis, Minn.: Univ. of Minnesota Press, 1964. [UMP]

BIOGRAPHICAL AND CRITICAL ESSAYS

15 BAUM, Bernard. "Willa Cather's Waste Land." *SAQ*, XLVIII (1949), 589–601. [Discusses Cather's anti-Semitism.]

16 BENNETT, Mildred R. "Willa Cather in Pittsburgh." *PrS*, XXXIII (1959), 64–76.

17 BRADFORD, Curtis. "Willa Cather's Uncollected Short Stories." *AL*, XXVI (1955), 537–551.

18 BROWN, E. K. "Homage to Willa Cather." *YR*, XXXVI (1946), 77–92. Also in 14.15.

1 BROWN, E. K. "Willa Cather and the West." *UTR*, V (1936), 444–466.

2 BULLOCK, Flora. "Willa Cather, Essayist and Dramatic Critic, 1891–1895." *PrS*, XXIII (1949), 393–401.

3 CONNOLLY, Francis X. "Willa Cather: Memory as Muse." See 13.4.

4 DAHL, Curtis. "An American *Georgic:* Willa Cather's *My Antonia.*" *CL*, VII (1955), 43–51.

5 EDEL, Leon. *Willa Cather, The Paradox of Success.* Washington, D.C.: Library of Congress, 1960. Also in 28.12. [A lecture delivered at the Library of Congress, Oct. 12, 1959.]

6 EDEL, Leon. "Willa Cather's *The Professor's House:* An Inquiry into the Use of Psychology in Literary Criticism." *I&P*, IV (1954), 66–79. Also in 13.10.

7 EDGAR, Pelham. "Two Anti-Realists: Willa Cather and Cabell." *The Art of the Novel.* New York: Macmillan, 1933, 255–267.

8 FOOTMAN, R. H. "The Genius of Willa Cather." *AL*, X (1938), 123–141.

9 GALE, Robert L. "Willa Cather and the Past." *SA*, IV (1958), 209–222.

10 GEISMAR, Maxwell. "Willa Cather: Lady in the Wilderness." See 5.17 and 28.12.

11 GIANNONE, Richard. "Music in *My Antonia.*" *PrS*, XXXVIII (1964), 346–361.

12 GREENE, George. "*Death Comes for the Archbishop.*" *NMQ*, XXVII (1958), 69–82.

13 HICKS, Granville. "The Case Against Willa Cather." *EJ*, XXII (1933), 703–710. Also in 28.12.

14 HINZ, John. "A Lost Lady and *The Professor's House.*" *VQR*, XXIX (1953), 70–85.

15 HINZ, John P. "The Real Alexander's Bridge." *AL* XXI (1950), 473–476.

16 HOFFMAN, Frederick J. "Willa Cather and Ellen Glasgow." See 4.10.

17 HOFFMAN, Frederick J. "Willa Cather's Two Worlds." See 6.10. [Mainly on *The Professor's House.*]

18 JACKS, L. V. "The Classics and Willa Cather." *PrS*, XXXV (1961), 289–296.

19 KAZIN, Alfred. "Elegy and Satire: Willa Cather and Ellen Glasgow." See 2.12 and 28.12.

20 KEELER, Clinton. "Narrative Without Accent: Willa Cather and Puvis de Chavannes." *AQ*, XVII (1965), 119–126.

21 KOHLER, Dayton. "Willa Cather: 1876–1947." *CE*, IX (1947), 8–18.

22 LEE, Robert Edson. "The Westerners: Willa Cather." *From West to East: Studies in the Literature of the American West.* Urbana, Ill.: Univ. of Illinois Press, 1966, 112–135. [Cather's shift to an "Eastern" viewpoint after 1913.]

1 MILLER, James E., Jr. "*My Ántonia:* A Frontier Drama of Time," *AQ*, X (1958), 476–484.

2 MORRIS, Lloyd. "Willa Cather." *NAR*, CCXIX (May, 1924), 641–652.

3 PORTER, Katherine Anne. "Reflections on Willa Cather." *The Days Before.* New York: Harcourt, Brace, 1952, 61–73.

4 RAPIN, René. "Willa Cather (1875–1947)." *EdL*, XXIII (1950), 39–50.

5 SCHROETER, James. "Willa Cather and *The Professor's House.*" *YR*, LIV (1965), 494–512. Also in 28.12.

6 SEIBEL, George. "Willa Cather from Nebraska." *NewC*, II (1949), 195–208. [Account of the Pittsburgh years.]

7 SHIVELY, James R. "Willa Cather Juvenilia." *PrS*, XXII (1948), 97–111.

8 TRILLING, Lionel. "Willa Cather." See 13.2 and 28.12.

9 WAGENKNECHT, Edward. "Willa Cather." *SR*, XXXVII (1929), 221–239.

10 WILLIAMS, Stanley T. "Some Spanish Influences on American Fiction: Mark Twain to Willa Cather." *Hispania*, XXXVI (1953), 133–136. [Emphasis on *Death Comes for the Archbishop* and *For Whom the Bell Tolls.*]

11 ZABEL, Morton Dauwen. "Willa Cather: The Tone of Time." In Zabel, *Craft and Character in Modern Fiction.* New York: Viking, 1957, 264–275. Also in 28.12.

Cozzens, James Gould (1903–   )

BIBLIOGRAPHY

12 LUDWIG, Richard M. "The Cozzens Papers." *PAW*, LVIII (May 30, 1958), 7–9, 13.

13 LUDWIG, Richard M. "James Gould Cozzens: A Review of Research and Criticism." *TSLL*, I (1959), 123–136.

14 LUDWIG, Richard M. "A Reading of the James Gould Cozzens Manuscripts." *PULC*, XIX (1957), 1–14.

15 MERIWETHER, James B. "A James Gould Cozzens Check List." *Crit*, I (1958), 57–63.

BIOGRAPHICAL AND CRITICAL BOOKS

16 BRACHER, Frederick. *The Novels of James Gould Cozzens.* New York: Harcourt, Brace, 1959.

17 HICKS, Granville. *James Gould Cozzens.* UMPAW, No. 58. Minneapolis, Minn.: Univ. of Minnesota Press, 1966. [UMP]

18 MAXWELL, D. E. S. *Cozzens.* Edinburgh: Oliver & Boyd, 1964.

1 MOONEY, Harry John, Jr. *James Gould Cozzens: Novelist of Intellect.* Pittsburgh, Pa.: Univ. of Pittsburgh Press, 1963. [Pitts]

BIOGRAPHICAL AND CRITICAL ESSAYS

2 COXE, Louis O. "Comments on Cozzens: A High Place." *Crit*, I (1958), 10–29.

3 COXE, Louis O. "The Complex World of James Gould Cozzens." *AL*, XXVII (1955), 157–171.

4 *Critique: Studies in Modern Fiction.* I, iii (1958). James Gould Cozzens Issue.

5 EISINGER, Chester E. "The Voice of Aggressive Aristocracy." *Midway*, No. 18 (1964), 100–128.

6 FERGUSSON, Francis. "Three Novels." *Perspectives USA*, No. 6 (1954), 30–44. [On *Guard of Honor*, comparing it with Warren's *All the King's Men* and Trilling's *The Middle of the Journey*.]

7 FROHOCK, W. M. "Cozzens and His Critics: A Problem in Perspective." *Strangers to this Ground.* Dallas, Tex.: Southern Methodist Univ. Press, 1961, 63–83.

8 HICKS, Granville. "The Reputation of James Gould Cozzens." *EJ*, XXXIX (1950), 1–7. *CE*, XI (1950), 177–183.

9 HOWE, Irving. "James Gould Cozzens: Novelist of the Republic." *NewR*, CXXXVIII (Jan. 20, 1958), 15–19.

10 HYMAN, Stanley Edgar. "James Gould Cozzens and the Art of the Possible." *NMQ*, XIX (1949), 476–498.

11 LYDENBERG, John. "Cozzens and His Critics." *CE*, XIX (1957), 99–104.

12 LYDENBERG, John. "Cozzens' Man of Responsibility." *Shenandoah*, X (1959), 11–18.

13 MACDONALD, Dwight. "By Cozzens Possessed: A Review of Reviews." *Commentary*, XXV (1958), 36–47. [A strong attack on Cozzens and his reviewers.]

14 MIZENER, Arthur. "The Undistorting Mirror." *KR*, XXVIII (1966), 595–611.

15 SCHOLES, Robert E. "The Commitment of James Gould Cozzens." *ArQ*, XVI (1960), 129–144.

16 WARD, John W. "James Gould Cozzens and the Condition of Modern Man." *ASch*, XXVII (1957), 92–99.

17 WATTS, Harold H. "James Gould Cozzens and the Genteel Tradition." *ColQ*, VI (1958), 257–273.

18 WEIMER, David R. "The Breath of Chaos in *The Just and the Unjust.* *Crit*, I (1958), 30–40.

Dos Passos, John (1896–)

BIBLIOGRAPHY

1 KALLICH, Martin. "Bibliography of John Dos Passos." *BB*, XIX (1949), 231–235.

2 POTTER, Jack. *John Dos Passos Bibliography*. Chicago: Normandie House, 1950.

3 REINHART, Virginia S. "John Dos Passos Bibliography: 1950–1966." *TCL*, XIII (1967), 167–178.

4 WHITE, William. "More Dos Passos Bibliographical Addenda." *PBSA*, XLV (1951), 156–158.

BIOGRAPHICAL AND CRITICAL BOOKS

5 DAVIS, Robert Gorham. *John Dos Passos*. UMPAW, No. 20. Minneapolis, Minn.: Univ. of Minnesota Press, 1962. [UMP]

6 DOS PASSOS, John. *The Best Times*. New York: New American Library, 1966. [Dos Passos's informal memoirs.]

7 WRENN, John H. *John Dos Passos*. New York: Twayne, 1961. [T-9-C&UPS]

BIOGRAPHICAL AND CRITICAL ESSAYS

8 ARDEN, Eugene. *"Manhattan Transfer:* An Experiment in Technique." *UKCR*, XXII (1955), 153–158.

9 BEACH, Joseph Warren. "Discontinuity: Dos Passos" and "Abstract Composition: Dos Passos." See 3.1.

10 BEACH, Joseph Warren. "Dos Passos: 1947." *SR*, LV (1947), 406–418.

11 BEACH, Joseph Warren. "John Dos Passos: The Artist in Uniform." and "John Dos Passos: Theory of the Leisure Class." See 5.5.

12 BORENSTEIN, Walter. "The Failure of Nerve: The Impact of Pio Baroja's Spain on John Dos Passos." *Nine Essays in Modern Literature*. Ed. by Donald E. Stanford. LSUSHS, No. 15. Baton Rouge, La.: Louisiana State Univ. Press, 1965, 63–87.

13 BROWN, Deming. "Dos Passos in Soviet Criticism." *CL*, V (1953), 332–350.

14 COWLEY, Malcolm. "Dos Passos: Poet Against the World." See 13.2.

15 COWLEY, Malcolm. "John Dos Passos: The Poet and the World." *NewR*, LXX (April 27, 1932), 303–305; LXXXVIII (Sept. 9, 1936), 34. Also in 14.15.

16 DEVOTO, Bernard. "John Dos Passos: Anatomist of Our Times." *SatRL*, XIV (Aug. 8, 1936), 3–4, 12–13.

17 DIGGINS, John P. "Dos Passos and Veblen's Villains." *AR*, XXIII (1963), 485–500.

1   FARRELL, James T. "Dos Passos and the Critics." *AMer*, XLVII (1939), 489–494.

2   FOOTMAN, R. H. "John Dos Passos." *SR*, XLVII (1939), 365–382.

3   FROHOCK, W. M. "John Dos Passos: Of Time and Frustration." *SWR*, XXXIII (1948), 71–80, 170–179.

4   GELFANT, Blanche. "John Dos Passos: The Synoptic Novel." See 9.6.

5   GELFANT, Blanche. "The Search for Identity in the Novels of John Dos Passos." *PMLA*, LXXVI (1961), 133–149.

6   GOLD, Michael. "The Education of John Dos Passos." *EJ*, XXII (1933), 87–97.

7   HICKS, Granville. "Dos Passos and His Critics." *AMer*, LXVIII (1949), 623–630.

8   HICKS, Granville. "Politics and John Dos Passos." *AR*, X (1950), 85–98.

9   KALLICH, Martin. "John Dos Passos, Fellow Traveller: A Dossier with Commentary." *TCL*, I (1956), 173–190.

10 KALLICH, Martin. "John Dos Passos: Liberty and the Father-Image." *AR*, X (1950), 99–106.

11 KAZIN, Alfred. "Into the Thirties: All the Lost Generations." Se 2.12.

12 KNOX, George. "Dos Passos and Painting." *TSLL*, VI (1964), 22–38.

13 KNOX, George. "Voice in the *U.S.A.* Biographies." *TSLL*, IV (1962), 109–116.

14 LANDSBERG, Melvin. "John R. Dos Passos: His Influence on the Novelist's Early Political Development." *AQ*, XVI (1964), 473–485. [Influence of Dos Passos's conservative father.]

15 LEAVIS, F. R. "A Serious Artist." *Scrutiny*, I (1932), 173–179.

16 LOWRY, E. A. "*Manhattan Transfer:* Dos Passos' Wasteland." *UR*, XXX (1963), 47–52.

17 LYDENBERG, John. "Dos Passos and the Ruined World." *PS*, VIII (1951), 16–23.

18 LYDENBERG, John. "Dos Passos's *U.S.A.:* The Words of the Hollow Men." *Essays on Determinism in American Literature.* Ed. by Sydney J. Krause. Kent, Ohio: Kent State Univ. Press, 1964, 97–107.

19 MC LUHAN, Herbert Marshall. "John Dos Passos: Technique vs. Sensibility." See 13.4 and 13.9.

20 RUGOFF, Milton. "Dos Passos: Novelist of Our Time." *SR*, XLIX (1941), 453–468.

21 RUOFF, Gene W. "Social Mobility and the Artist in *Manhattan Transfer* and *The Music of Time.*" *WSCL*, V (1964), 64–76.

22 SANDERS, David. "The 'Anarchism' of John Dos Passos." *SAQ*, LX (1961), 44–55.

23 SANDERS, David. "Interview with John Dos Passos." *ClareQ*, XI (1964), 89–100.

1 SANDERS, David. "Lies and the System: Enduring Themes from Dos Passos's Early Novels." *SAQ*, LXV (1966), 215–228.

2 SCHWARTZ, Delmore. "John Dos Passos and the Whole Truth." *SoR*, IV (1938), 351–367.

3 SMITH, James S. "The Novelist of Discomfort: A Reconsideration of John Dos Passos." *CE*, XIX (1958), 332–338.

4 STOLTZFUS, Ben. "John Dos Passos and the French." *CL*, XV (1963), 146–163.

5 TRILLING, Lionel. "The America of John Dos Passos." *PR*, IV (1938), 26–32.

6 VAN GELDER, Robert. "An Interview with John Dos Passos. See 14.9.

7 WADE, Mason. "Novelist of America: John Dos Passos." *NAR*, CCXLIV (1937), 349–367.

Ellison, Ralph (1914–   )

TEXTS

8 *Shadow and Act*. New York: Random House, 1964. [A selection of Ellison's essays.] [Q3022-Sig]

BIOGRAPHICAL AND CRITICAL ESSAYS

9 BAUMBACH, Jonathan. "Nightmare of A Native Son: Ralph Ellison's *Invisible Man*." *Crit*, VI, i (1963). 48–65. Also in 5.4.

10 BENNETT, John Z. "The Race and the Runner: Ellison's *Invisible Man*." *XUS*, V(1966), 12–26.

11 BONE, Robert A. "Ralph Ellison and the Uses of Imagination." See 10.2.

12 BONE, Robert A. See 7.18.

13 CHESTER, Alfred and Vilma HOWARD. "Ralph Ellison." See 13.16. [A *Paris Review* Interview.]

14 ELLISON, Ralph. "Hidden Name and Complex Fate: A Writer's Experience in the United States." In Ralph Ellison and Karl Shapiro, *The Writer's Experience*. Washington, D.C.: Library of Congress, 1964, 1–15.

15 ELLISON, Ralph. "On Becoming a Writer." *Commentary*, XXXVIII (1964), 57–60.

16 GELLER, Allen. "An Interview with Ralph Ellison." *TamR*, No. 32 (1964), 3–24.

17 GLICKSBERG, Charles I. "The Symbolism of Vision." *SWR*, XXXIX (1954), 259–265.

18 HYMAN, Stanley Edgar and Ralph ELLISON. "The Negro Writer in America: An Exchange." *PR*, XXV (1958), 197–222.

1 KLEIN, Marcus. "Ralph Ellison." See 6.14.

2 KNOX, George. "The Negro Novelist's Sensibility and the Outsider Theme." *WHR*, XI (1957), 137–148. [On *Invisible Man* and Richard Wright's *The Outsider*.]

3 KOSTELANETZ, Richard. "The Politics of Ellison's Booker: *Invisible Man* as Symbolic History." *ChiR*, XIX, ii (1967), 5–26.

4 LEHAN, Richard. "The Strange Silence of Ralph Ellison." *CEJ*, I (1965), 63–68.

5 MARCUS, Steven. See 11.4.

6 OLDERMAN, Raymond M. "Ralph Ellison's Blues and *Invisible Man*." *WSCL*, VII (1966), 142–159.

7 RANDALL, John H., III. "Ralph Ellison: *Invisible Man*." *RLV*, XXXI (1965), 24–45.

8 ROVIT, Earl H. "Ralph Ellison and the American Comic Tradition." *WSCL*, I (1960), 34–42. Also in 14.10.

9 THOMPSON, James, Lennox RAPHAEL, and Steve CANNON. " 'A Very Stern Discipline': An Interview with Ralph Ellison." *Harpers*, CCXXXIV (Mar., 1967), 76–95.

10 WEST, Anthony. "Ralph Ellison." *Principles and Persuasions*. New York: Harcourt, Brace, 1957, 212–219.

Farrell, James T. (1904–   )

BIBLIOGRAPHY

11 BRANCH, Edgar M. *A Bibliography of James T. Farrell's Writings, 1921–1957*. Philadelphia, Pa.: Univ. of Pennsylvania Press, 1959.

12 BRANCH, Edgar M. "A Supplement to the Bibliography of James T. Farrell's Writings." *ABC*, XI (1961), 42–48.

13 BRANCH, Edgar M. "Bibliography of James T. Farrell: A Supplement." *ABC*, XVII, ix (1967), 9–19.

BIOGRAPHICAL AND CRITICAL BOOKS

14 BRANCH, Edgar M. *James T. Farrell*. UMPAW, No. 29. Minneapolis, Minn.: Univ. of Minnesota Press, 1963. [UMP]

BIOGRAPHICAL AND CRITICAL ESSAYS

15 ALDRIDGE, John W. "The Education of James T. Farrell." See 12.15.

16 ALEXIS, Gerhard T. "Farrell Since *Our* Days of Anger." *CE*, XXVII (1965), 221–226.

17 BEACH, Joseph Warren. "James T. Farrell: Tragedy of the Poolroom Loafer" and "James T. Farrell: The Plight of the Children." See 5.5.

18 BIRNEY, Earle. "The Fiction of James T. Farrell." *CF*, XIX (1939), 21–24.

1   BRANCH, Edgar M. "Destiny, Culture, and Technique: *Studs Lonigan*." *UKCR*, XXIX (1962), 103–113.

2   BRANCH, Edgar M. "Freedom and Determinism in James T. Farrell's Fiction." *Essays on Determinism in American Literature*. Ed. by Sydney J. Krause. Kent, Ohio: Kent State Univ. Press, 1964, 79–96.

3   BRANCH, Edgar M. "*Studs Lonigan*, Symbolism and Theme." *CE*, XXIII (1961), 191–196.

4   CARGILL, Oscar. See 2.7.

5   DOUGLAS, Wallace. "The Case of James T. Farrell." *TriQ*, No. 2 (1965), 105–123.

6   FARRELL, James T. "Farrell Revisits Studs Lonigan's Neighborhood." *NYTBR*, June 20, 1954, 4–5, 12.

7   FARRELL, James T. "An Introduction to Two Novels." *UKCR*, XIII (1947), 217–224. [The novels are *A World I Never Made* and *No Star is Lost*.]

8   FARRELL, James T. "A Note on Future Plans." *TriQ*, No. 2 (1965), 139–140.

9   FARRELL, James T. "A Novelist Begins." *Atlantic*, CXLII (1938), 330–334.

10 FARRELL, James T. "Reflections at Fifty." *Perspectives, USA*, No. 14 (1956), 26–32.

11 FROHOCK, W. M. "James Farrell, The Precise Content." *SWR*, XXXV (1950), 39–48. Repr. in 9.4.

12 GELFANT, Blanche. "James T. Farrell: The Ecological Novel." See 9.6.

13 GRATTAN, C. Harley. "James T. Farrell, Moralist." *Harper's*, CCIX (Oct., 1954), 93–94, 96, 98.

14 GREGORY, Horace. "James T. Farrell: Beyond the Provinces of Art." *New World Writing*. Fifth Mentor Selection (1954), 52–65.

15 HATFIELD, Ruth. "The Intellectual Honesty of James T. Farrell." *CE*, III (1942), 337–346.

16 HOWE, Irving. "James T. Farrell: The Critic Calcified." *PR*, XIV (1947), 545–546, 548, 550, 552.

17 KLIGERMAN, Jack. "The Quest for Self: James T. Farrell's Character Bernard Carr." *UKCR*, XXIX (1962), 9–16.

18 LOVETT, Robert Morss. "James T. Farrell." *EJ*, XXVI (1937), 347–354.

19 MITCHELL, Richard. "*Studs Lonigan:* Research in Morality." *CentR*, VI (1962), 202–214.

20 O'MALLEY, Frank. "James T. Farrell: Two Twilight Images." See 13.4.

21 ROSENTHAL, T. G. "Studs Lonigan and the Search for an American Tragedy." *BAASB*, No. 7 (1963), 46–54.

22 STOCK, Irvin. "Farrell and His Critics." *ArQ*, VI (1950), 328–338.

1 VAN GELDER, Robert. "An Interview with James T. Farrell." See 14.9.

2 WALCUTT, Charles Child. "James T. Farrell and the Reversible Topcoat." *ArQ*, VII (1952), 293–310.

3 WALCUTT, Charles Child. "James T. Farrell: Aspects of Telling the Whole Truth." See 12.9.

4 WALCUTT, Charles Child. "Naturalism in 1946: Dreiser and Farrell." *Accent*, VI (1946), 263–267.

5 WILLINGHAM, Calder. "Note on James T. Farrell." *QRL*, II (1946), 120–124.

Faulkner, William (1897–1962)

TEXTS

6 COLLINS, Carvel, ed. *New Orleans Sketches*. With introd. New York: Random House, 1968. [Early Faulkner pieces from the New Orleans *Times-Picayune* and *The Double Dealer*.]

7 COLLINS, Carvel, ed. *William Faulkner: Early Prose and Poetry*. Boston: Little, Brown, 1962. [Covers 1919–1925.]

8 COWLEY, Malcolm, ed. The *Portable Faulkner*. With introd. New York: Viking, 1946.

9 FANT, Joseph L., III and Robert ASHLEY, eds. *Faulkner at West Point*. New York: Random House, 1964. [Transcript of Faulkner's 1962 lectures, conferences.]

10 GWYNN, Frederick L. and Joseph L. BLOTNER, eds. *Faulkner in the University: Class Conferences at the University of Virginia, 1957–1958*. Charlottesville, Va.: Univ. of Virginia Press, 1959.

11 JELLIFFE, Robert A., ed. *Faulkner at Nagano*. Tokyo: Kenkyusha, Ltd., 1956. [Transcripts of Faulkner's interviews, seminars, statements during a 1955 visit to Japan.]

12 MERIWETHER, James B., ed. *Essays, Speeches, and Public Letters of William Faulkner*. New York: Random House, 1965.

BIBLIOGRAPHY

13 ARCHER, H. Richard. "The Writings of William Faulkner: A Challenge to the Bibliographer." *PBSA*, L (1956), 229–242.

14 BEEBE, Maurice. "Criticism of William Faulkner: A Selected Checklist." *MFS*, XIII, i (1967), 115–161.

15 LONGLEY, John L. and Robert DANIEL. "Faulkner's Critics: A Selective Bibliography." *Perspective*, III (1950), 202–208.

16 MERIWETHER, James B. "Notes on the Textual History of *The Sound and the Fury*." *PBSA*, LVI (1962), 285–316.

1 MERIWETHER, James B. "Some Notes on the Text of Faulkner's *Sanctuary*." *PBSA*, LV (1961), 192–206.

2 MERIWETHER, James B. "The Text of Faulkner's Books: An Introduction and Some Notes." *MFS*, IX (1963), 159–170.

3 MERIWETHER, James B. "William Faulkner: A Check List." *PULC*, XVIII (1957), 136–158.

4 SLEETH, Irene Lynn. *William Faulkner: A Bibliography of Criticism.* Denver, Colo.: Alan Swallow, 1962.

BIOGRAPHICAL AND CRITICAL BOOKS

5 BACKMAN, Melvin. *Faulkner, The Major Years: A Critical Study.* Bloomington, Ind.: Indiana Univ. Press, 1966. [MB-89-Ind]

6 BECK, Warren. *Man in Motion: Faulkner's Trilogy.* Madison, Wisc.: Univ. of Wisconsin Press, 1961. [W-25-UWis.]

7 BLOTNER, Joseph, comp. *William Faulkner's Library—A Catalogue.* Charlottesville, Va.: Univ. of Virginia Press, 1965.

8 BROOKS, Cleanth. *William Faulkner: The Yoknapatawpha Country.* New Haven, Conn.: Yale Univ. Press, 1963. [Y170-Yale]

9 CAMPBELL, Harry Modean and Ruel E. FOSTER. *William Faulkner.* Norman, Okla.: Univ. of Oklahoma Press, 1951.

10 COUGHLAN, Robert. *The Private World of William Faulkner.* New York: Harper, 1953. [G1144-Avon]

11 COWLEY, Malcolm. *The Faulkner-Cowley File: Letters and Memories, 1944–1962.* New York: Viking, 1966.

12 CULLEN, John B. and Floyd C. WATKINS. *Old Times in the Faulkner Country.* Chapel Hill, N.C.: Univ. of North Carolina Press, 1961. [Reminiscences of Cullen, hunting companion and fellow townsman of Faulkner.]

13 DOWNER, Alan S., ed. *English Institute Essays.* New York: Columbia Univ. Press, 1952. [Papers on Faulkner by various hands.]

14 FALKNER, Murry C. *The Falkners of Mississippi: A Memoir.* Baton Rouge, La.: Louisiana State Univ. Press, 1967. [By Faulkner's brother.]

15 FAULKNER, John. *My Brother Bill: An Affectionate Reminiscence.* New York: Trident Press, 1963. [50018-PB]

16 FORD, Margaret P. and Suzanne KINCAID. *Who's Who in Faulkner.* Baton Rouge, La.: Louisiana State Univ. Press, 1963. [L-7-LSU]

17 GOLD, Joseph. *William Faulkner: A Study in Humanism, From Metaphor to Discourse.* Norman, Okla.: Univ. of Oklahoma Press, 1966.

18 HOFFMAN, Frederick J. *William Faulkner.* New York: Twayne, 1961. [T-1-C&UPS]

19 HOFFMAN, Frederick J. and Olga W. VICKERY, eds. *William Faulkner: Three Decades of Criticism.* East Lansing, Mich.: Mich. State Univ. Press, 1960. [Essays by various hands.] [HO-19-Hbgr]

20 HOWE, Irving. *William Faulkner: A Critical Study.* 2nd ed. New York: Random House, 1962. [V-213-Vin]

1 HUNT, John W. *William Faulkner: Art in Theological Tension*, Syracuse, N.Y.: Syracuse Univ. Press, 1965.

2 KIRK, Robert W. and Marvin KLOTZ. *Faulkner's People: A Complete Guide and Index to Characters in the Fiction of William Faulkner.* Berkeley, Calif.: Univ. of California Press, 1963. [Cal-107-Calif]

3 LONGLEY, John L., Jr. *The Tragic Mask: A Study of Faulkner's Heroes.* Chapel Hill, N.C.: Univ. of North Carolina Press, 1963. [Chb-5-UNC]

4 MALIN, Irving. *William Faulkner: An Interpretation.* Stanford, Calif.: Stanford Univ. Press, 1957.

5 MILLGATE, Michael. *The Achievement of William Faulkner.* New York: Random House, 1966.

6 MILLGATE, Michael. *William Faulkner.* New York: Grove Press, 1961.

7 MINER, Ward L. *The World of William Faulkner.* Durham, N.C.: Duke Univ. Press, 1952. [E142-Ever]

8 NILON, Charles H. *Faulkner and the Negro.* New York: Citadel, 1965. [C200-Ctdl]

9 O'CONNOR, William Van. *The Tangled Fire of William Faulkner.* Minneapolis, Minn.: Univ. of Minnesota Press, 1954.

10 O'CONNOR, William Van. *William Faulkner.* UMPAW, No. 3. Minneapolis, Minn.: Univ. of Minnesota Press, 1959 [UMP]

11 RUNYAN, Harry. *A Faulkner Glossary.* New York: Citadel, 1964.

12 SLATOFF, Walter J. *Quest for Failure: A Study of William Faulkner.* Ithaca, N.Y.: Cornell Univ. Press, 1960.

13 SWIGGART, Peter. *The Art of Faulkner's Novels.* Austin, Tex.: Univ. of Texas Press, 1962.

14 THOMPSON, Lawrance. *William Faulkner: An Introduction and Interpretation.* 2nd ed. New York: Holt, Rinehart & Winston, 1967.

15 VICKERY, Olga W. *The Novels of William Faulkner, A Critical Interpretation.* Rev. ed. Baton Rouge, La.: Louisiana State Univ. Press, 1964.

16 VOLPE, Edmond L. *A Reader's Guide to William Faulkner.* New York: Noonday Press, 1964. [N255-Noon]

17 WAGGONER, Hyatt H. *William Faulkner: From Jefferson to the World.* Lexington, Ky.: Univ. of Kentucky Press, 1959. [108-UKP]

18 WARREN, Robert Penn, ed. *Faulkner: A Collection of Critical Essays.* Englewood Cliffs, N.J.: Prentice-Hall, 1966. [S-TC-65-Spec]

19 WEBB, James W. and A. Wigfall GREEN. *William Faulkner of Oxford.* Baton Rouge, La.: Louisiana State Univ. Press, 1965. [Reminiscences of Faulkner by Oxford friends.]

20 WOODRUFF, Neal, Jr., ed. *Studies in Faulkner.* CaSE, VI. Pittsburgh, Pa.: Carnegie Institute of Technology, 1961. [Essays by various hands.]

BIOGRAPHICAL AND CRITICAL ESSAYS

1 ABEL, Darrel. "Frozen Movement in *Light in August*." *BUSE*, III (1957), 32–44.

2 ADAMS, Richard P. "The Apprenticeship of William Faulkner." *TSE*, XII (1963), 113–156.

3 ADAMS, Robert M. "Poetry in the Novel: or Faulkner Esemplastic." *VQR*, XXIX (1953), 419–434. [Coleridge and Faulkner.]

4 AIKEN, Conrad. "William Faulkner: The Novel as Form." *Atlantic*, CLXIV (1939), 650–654. Also in 38.19 and 39.18.

5 ALTENBERND, Lynn. "A Suspended Moment: The Irony of History in William Faulkner's 'The Bear'." *MLN*, LXXV (1960), 572–582.

6 ALTER, Jean V. "Faulkner, Sartre, and the 'nouveau roman'." *Symposium*, XX (1966), 101–112.

7 ARTHOS, John. "Ritual and Humor in the Writing of William Faulkner." *Accent*, IX (1948), 17–30.

8 BACKMAN, Melvin. "Faulkner's Sick Heroes: Bayard Sartoris and Quentin Compson." *MFS*, II (1956), 95–108.

9 BACKMAN, Melvin. "Sickness and Primitivism: A Dominant Pattern in William Faulkner's Work." *Accent*, XIV (1954), 61–73.

10 BACKMAN, Melvin. "Sutpen and the South: A Study of *Absalom, Absalom!*" *PMLA*, LXXX (1965), 596–604.

11 BACKMAN, Melvin. "The Wilderness and the Negro in Faulkner's 'The Bear'." *PMLA*, LXXVI (1961), 595–600.

12 BAKER, Carlos. "William Faulkner: The Doomed and the Damned." See 13.1.

13 BALDANZA, Frank. "Faulkner and Stein: A Study in Stylistic Intransigence." *GaR*, XIII (1959), 274–286.

14 BALDWIN, James. "Faulkner and Desegregation." *PR*, XXIII (1956), 568–573.

15 BEACH, Joseph Warren. "William Faulkner: The Haunted South." and "William Faulkner: Virtuoso." See 5.5.

16 BECK, Warren. "Faulkner and the South." *AR*, I (1941), 82–94.

17 BECK, Warren. "Faulkner's Point of View." *CE*, II (1941), 736–749.

18 BECK, Warren. "William Faulkner's Style." *APref*, IV (1941), 195–211. Also in 39.18.

19 BERLAND, Alwyn. "*Light in August:* The Calvinism of William Faulkner." *MFS*, VIII (1962), 159–170.

20 BJORK, Lennart. "Ancient Myths and the Moral Framework of Faulkner's *Absalom, Absalom!*" *AL*, XXXV (1963), 196–204.

21 BOUVARD, Löic. "Conversation with William Faulkner." Trans. by Henry Dan Piper. *MFS*, V (1959), 361–364.

1 BOWLING, Lawrence E. "Faulkner and the Theme of Innocence." *KR*, XX (1958), 466–487.

2 BOWLING, Lawrence E. "Faulkner and the Theme of Isolation." *GaR*, XVIII (1964), 50–66.

3 BOWLING, Lawrence E. "Faulkner: Technique of *The Sound and the Fury*." *KR*, X (1948), 552–566.

4 BRADFORD, Melvin E. "Faulkner, James Baldwin, and the South." *GaR*, XX (1966), 431–443.

5 BRENNAN, Dan. "Journey South." *UKCR*, XXII (1955), 11–16. [Account of a visit with Faulkner in 1940.]

6 BROOKS, Cleanth. "*Absalom, Absalom!:* The Definition of Innocence." *SR*, LIX (1951), 543–558.

7 BROOKS, Cleanth. "Faulkner's Vision of Good and Evil." *MR*, III (1962), 692–712.

8 BROOKS, Cleanth. "Primitivism in *The Sound and the Fury*." See 38.13.

9 BRUMM, Ursula. "Wilderness and Civilization: A Note on William Faulkner." *PR*, XXII (1955), 340–350. [On Faulkner's primitivism.]

10 BURGUM, Edwin Berry. "William Faulkner's Patterns of American Decadence." See 8.4.

11 CAMPBELL, Harry Modean. "Experiment and Achievement." *SR*, LI (1943), 305–320.

12 CAMPBELL, Harry Modean. "Structural Devices in the Works of Faulkner." *Perspective*, III (1950), 209–226.

13 CANTWELL, Robert. "The Faulkners: Recollections of a Gifted Family." *New World Writing*. Second Mentor Selection (1952), 300–315.

14 CARTER, Hodding. "Faulkner and His Folk." *PULC*, XVIII (1957), 95–107.

15 CHASE, Richard. "The Stone and the Crucifixion: Faulkner's *Light in August*." *KR*, X (1948), 539–551.

16 COINDREAU, Maurice Edgar. "The Faulkner I Knew." *Shenandoah*, XVI, ii (1965), 27–35. [By Faulkner's French translator.]

17 COINDREAU, Maurice Edgar. "On Translating Faulkner." *PULC*, XVIII (1957), 108–113.

18 COINDREAU, Maurice Edgar. "William Faulkner in France." *YFS*, No. 10 (1953), 85–91.

19 COLLINS, Carvel. "Faulkner and Certain Earlier Southern Fiction." *CE*, XVI (1954), 92–97.

20 COLLINS, Carvel. "The Interior Monologues of *The Sound and the Fury*." *EIE, 1952*. New York: Columbia Univ. Press, 1954. Also in 13.10.

21 COLLINS, Carvel. "The Pairing of *The Sound and the Fury* and *As I Lay Dying*." *PULC*, XVIII (1957), 114–123.

22 COLLINS, Carvel. "William Faulkner, *The Sound and the Fury*." See 14.7.

1 COTTRELL, Beekman W. "Christian Symbols in *Light in August*." *MFS*, II (Winter, 1956), 207–213.

2 COWLEY, Malcolm. "Introduction." *The Portable Faulkner*. New York: Viking, 1946. [A landmark in Faulkner criticism.]

3 CROSS, Barbara M. "Apocalypse and Comedy in *As I Lay Dying*." *TSLL*, III (1961), 251–258.

4 CROSS, Barbara M. "*The Sound and the Fury:* The Pattern of Sacrifice." *ArQ*, XVI (1960), 5–16.

5 DAUNER, Louise. "Quentin and the Walking Shadow: The Dilemma of Nature and Culture." *ArQ*, XXI (1965), 159–171.

6 DOMINICUS, A. M. "An Interview with Faulkner." *FaS*, III (1954), 33–37.

7 DOUGLAS, Harold J. and Robert DANIEL. "Faulkner and the Puritanism of the South." *TSL*, II (1957), 1–13.

8 EBY, Cecil D. "Faulkner and the Southwestern Humorists." *Shenandoah*, XI (1959), 13–21.

9 EDEL, Leon. "How to Read *The Sound and the Fury*." *Varieties of Literary Experience*. Ed. by Stanley Burnshaw. New York: New York Univ. Press, 1962, 241–257.

10 FALKNER, Murry C. "The Falkners of Oxford: The Enchanted Years." *SoR*, III (1967), 357–386.

11 FARNHAM, James F. "Faulkner's Unsung Hero: Gavin Stevens." *ArQ*, XXI (1965), 115–132.

12 FAULKNER, William. "Mississippi." *Holiday*, XV (1954), 35–46. [Contains autobiographical information.]

13 FISHER, Richard E. "The Wilderness, the Commissary, and the Bedroom: Faulkner's Ike McCaslin as Hero in a Vacuum." *ES*, XLIV (1963), 19–28.

14 FLINT, R. W. "Faulkner as Elegist." *HudR*, VII (1954), 246–257.

15 FOSTER, Ruel E. "Dream as Symbolic Act in Faulkner." *Perspective*, II (1949), 179–194.

16 FRANKLIN, Rosemary. "Animal Magnetism in *As I Lay Dying*." *AQ*, XVIII (1966), 24–34.

17 FRAZIER, David L. "Gothicism in *Sanctuary:* The Black Pall and The Crap Table." *MFS*, II (1956), 114–124.

18 FROHOCK, W. M. "William Faulkner: The Private Versus the Public Vision." *SWR*, XXXIV (1949), 281–294.

19 GALHARN, Carl. "Faulkner's Faith: Roots from *The Wild Palms*." *TCL*, I (1955), 139–160.

20 GARRETT, George. "Faulkner's Early Literary Criticism." *TSLL*, I (1959), 3–10.

21 GERARD, Albert. "Justice in Yoknapatawpha County: Some Symbolic Motifs in Faulkner's Later Writing." *FaS*, II (1954), 49–57.

22 GILLEY, Leonard. "The Wilderness Theme in Faulkner's 'The Bear'." *MQ*, VI (1965), 379–385.

1 GOLD, Joseph. "Delusion and Redemption in Faulkner's *A Fable*." *MFS*, VII (1961), 145–156.

2 GREENE, Graham. "The Furies of Mississippi." *LoM*, XXXV (1937), 517–518.

3 GREER, Scott. "Joe Christmas and the 'Social Self'." *MissQ*, XI (1958) 160–166. [Cautions against sociological readings of Faulkner.]

4 GREET, T. Y. "The Theme and Structure of Faulkner's *The Hamlet*." *PMLA*, LXXII (1957), 775–790.

5 GRENIER, Cynthia. "The Art of Fiction: An Interview with William Faulkner—Sept., 1955." *Accent*, XVI (1956), 167–177.

6 GWYNN, Frederick L. "Faulkner's Raskolnikov." *MFS*, IV (1958), 169–172. [Raskolnikov and Quentin Compson.]

7 GWYNN, Frederick L. and Joseph L. BLOTNER, eds. "Faulkner on Dialect." *UVM*, II (1958), 7–13, 32–37.

8 HAFLEY, James. "Faulkner's *Fable:* Dream and Transfiguration." *Accent*, XVI (1956), 3–14.

9 HAMILTON, Edith. "Faulkner: Sorcerer or Slave?" *SatR*, XXXV (1951), 19, 41–42. [An adverse view of Faulkner.]

10 HANDY, William J. "*As I Lay Dying:* Faulkner's Inner Reporter." *KR*, XXI (1959), 437–451. Also in 14.11.

11 HARDWICK, Elizabeth. "Faulkner and the South Today." *PR*, XV (1948), 1130–1135. Also in 39.18. [A review-essay.]

12 HOADLEY, Frank M. "Folk Humor in the Novels of William Faulkner." *TFSB*, XXIII (1957) 75–82.

13 HOLMAN, C. Hugh. "The Unity of Faulkner's *Light in August*." *PMLA*, LXXIII (1958), 155–166.

14 HOPKINS, Viola. "William Faulkner's *The Hamlet:* A Study in Meaning and Form." *Accent*, XV (1955), 125–144.

15 HOWE, Irving. "William Faulkner and the Negroes." *Commentary*, XII (1951), 359–367.

16 HUGHES, Richard. "Faulkner and Bennett." *Encounter*, XXI (1963), 59–61. [On Faulkner's English debut.]

17 HUMPHREY, Robert. "Form and Function of Stream of Consciousness in William Faulkner's *The Sound and the Fury*." *UKCR*, XIX (1952), 24–40.

18 JACOBS, Robert D. "Faulkner's Tragedy of Isolation." *HoR*, VI (1953), 162–183.

19 JACOBS, Robert D. "William Faulkner: The Passion and the Penance." See 14.3.

20 JENSEN, Eric G., S.J. "The Play Element in Faulkner's 'The Bear'." *TSLL*, VI (1964), 170–187.

21 JEWKES, W. T. "Counterpoint in Faulkner's *The Wild Palms*." *WSCL*, II (1961), 39–53.

22 JUSTUS, James H. "The Epic Design of *Absalom, Absalom!*" *TSLL*, IV (1962), 157–176.

23 KARTIGANER, Donald M. "Faulkner's *Absalom, Absalom!:* The Discovery of Values." *AL*, XXXVII (1965), 291–306.

1 KARTIGANER, Donald M. "The Role of Myth in *Absalom, Absalom!*" *MFS*, IX (1963), 357–369.

2 KAZIN, Alfred. "The Rhetoric and the Agony." See 2.12. [A skeptical view of Faulkner.]

3 KAZIN, Alfred. "The Stillness of *Light in August*." *PR*, XXIV (1957), 519–538. Also in 14.5 and 39.18.

4 KING, Roma A., Jr. "Everyman's Warfare: A Study of Faulkner's *Fable*." *MFS*, II (1956), 132–138.

5 KLOTZ, Marvin. "Procrustean Revision in Faulkner's *Go Down, Moses*." *AL*, XXXVII (1965), 1–16.

6 KOHLER, Dayton. "*A Fable:* The Novel as Myth." *CE*, XVI (1955), 471–478.

7 KOHLER, Dayton. "William Faulkner and the Social Conscience." *CE*, XI (1949), 119–127; *EJ*, XXXVIII (1949), 542–552.

8 KUBIE, Lawrence S. "William Faulkner's *Sanctuary:* An Analysis." *SatRL*, XI (Oct. 20, 1934), 218, 224–226. Also in 39.18.

9 LA BUDDE, Kenneth. "Cultural Primitivism in William Faulkner's 'The Bear'," *AQ*, II (1950), 322–328.

10 LAMONT, William H. F. "The Chronology of *Light in August*." *MFS*, III (1957) 360–361. [Corrects earlier misconceptions.]

11 LANGSTON, Beach. "The Meaning of Lena Grove and Gail Hightower in *Light in August*." *BUSE*, V (1961), 46–63.

12 LAWSON, Lewis A. "The Grotesque-Comic in the Snopes Trilogy." *L&P*, XV (1965), 107–119.

13 LEHAN, Richard. "Faulkner's Poetic Prose: Style and Meaning in 'The Bear'." *CE*, XXVII (1965), 243–247.

14 LEIBOWITZ, Herbert A. "The Snopes Dilemma and the South." *UKCR*, XXVIII (1962), 273–284.

15 LEWIS, R. W. B. "William Faulkner: The Hero in the New World." *The Picaresque Saint*. Philadelphia, Pa.: Lippincott, 1959. Also in 39.18. [KB28-Key]

16 LEWIS, Wyndham. "A Moralist with a Corn Cob." *L&L*, XVI (1934), 312–318.

17 LIND, Ilse D. "The Calvinistic Burden of *Light in August*." *NEQ*, XXX (1957), 307–329.

18 LIND, Ilse. "The Design and Meaning of *Absalom, Absalom!*" *PMLA*, LXX (1955), 887–912.

19 LISCA, Peter. "*The Hamlet:* Genesis and Revisions." *FaS*, III (1954), 5–13.

20 LISCA, Peter. "Some New Light on Faulkner's *Sanctuary*." *FaS*, II (1953), 5–9.

21 LONGLEY, John L., Jr. "Joe Christmas: The Hero in the Modern World." *VQR*, XXXIII (1957), 233–249. Also in 39.3 and 39.18.

22 LOWREY, Perrin. "Concepts of Time in *The Sound and the Fury*." *FIE* (1952), 57–82.

1   LYDENBERG, John. "Nature Myth in Faulkner's 'The Bear'." *AL*, XXIV (1952), 62–72.

2   LYTLE, Andrew. "Regeneration for the Man." *SR*, LVII (1949), 120–127. Also in 39.18.

3   LYTLE, Andrew. "The Son of Man: He Will Prevail." *SR*, LXIII (1955), 114–137. [An analysis of *A Fable*.]

4   LYTLE, Andrew. "*The Town:* Helen's Last Stand." *SR*, LXV (1957), 475–484.

5   MAGNY, Claude-Edmonde. "Faulkner or Theological Inversion." See 39.18.

6   MARCOVIĆ, Vida. "Interview with Faulkner." *TSLL*, V (1964), 463–466.

7   MC CLENNEN, Joshua. "*Absalom, Absalom!* and the Meaning of History." *PMASAL*, XLII (1956), 357–369.

8   MERIWETHER, James B. "Early Notices of Faulkner by Phil Stone and Louis Cochran." *MissQ*, XVII (1964), 136–164.

9   MILLER, Douglas T. "Faulkner and the Civil War: Myth and Reality." *AQ*, XV (1963), 200–209.

10   MILLGATE, Michael. " 'A Fair Job': A Study of Faulkner's *Sanctuary*." *REL*, IV (1963), 47–62.

11   MILLS, Ralph J., Jr. "Faulkner's Essential Vision: Notes on *A Fable*." *ChS*, XLIV (1961), 187–198.

12   MOLONEY, Michael F. "The Enigma of Time: Proust, Virginia Woolf, and Faulkner." *Thought*, XXXII (1957), 69–85.

13   MONTEIRO, George. "Bankruptcy in Time: A Reading of William Faulkner's *Pylon*." *TCL*, IV (1958), 9–20.

14   MORRIS, Wright. "The Function of Rage: William Faulkner." See 13.14.

15   MOSES, W. R. "The Unity of *The Wild Palms*." *MFS*, II (1956), 125–131.

16   MOSES, W. R. "Where History Crosses Myth: Another Reading of 'The Bear'." *Accent*, XIII (1953), 21–33.

17   MUSTE, John M. "The Failure of Love in *Go Down, Moses*." *MFS*, X (1964), 366–378.

18   NESTRICK, William V. "The Function of Form in *The Bear*, Section IV." *TCL*, XII (1966), 131–137.

19   O'CONNOR, William Van. "The Wilderness Theme in Faulkner's 'The Bear'." *Accent*, XIII (1953), 12–20.

20   O'DONNELL, George M. "Faulkner's Mythology." *KR*, I (1939), 285–299. Also in 39.18.

21   O'FAOLAIN, Sean. "William Faulkner, or More Genius Than Talent." *The Vanishing Hero: Studies in Novelists of the Twenties*. London: Eyre & Spottiswoode, 1956, 99–134. [43-UL]

22   PATERSON, John. "Hardy, Faulkner, and the Prosaics of Tragedy." *CRAS*, V (1961), 156–175. [With special reference to *The Mayor of Casterbridge* and *Absalom, Absalom!*]

23   PEARCE, Richard. "Faulkner's One Ring Circus." *WSCL*, VII (1966), 270–283. [On *Light in August*.]

1 PERLUCK, Herbert A. "The Heart's Driving Complexity: An Unromantic Reading of Faulkner's 'The Bear'." *Accent*, XX (1960), 23–46.

2 PODHORETZ, Norman. "William Faulkner and the Problem of War: His Fable of Faith." *Commentary*, XVIII (1954), 227–232. Also in 39.18. [A review.]

3 POIRIER, William. "Strange Gods in Jefferson, Mississippi." *SR*, LIII (1945), 44–56.

4 POUILLON, Jean. "Time and Destiny in Faulkner." See 39.18.

5 PRITCHETT, V. S. "Time Frozen: *A Fable*." *PR*, XXI (1954), 557–561. [A review.]

6 RICHARDSON, H. Edward. "The 'Hemingwaves' in Faulkner's *Wild Palms*." *MFS*, IV (1958), 357–360.

7 RICHARDSON, H. Edward. "The Ways that Faulkner Walked: A Pilgrimage." *ArQ*, XXI (1965), 133–145. [Interview with Phil Stone; impressions of Oxford.]

8 RIEDEL, F. C. "Faulkner as Stylist." *SAQ*, LVI (1957), 462–479.

9 ROBERTS, James L. "The Individual and the Family: Faulkner's *As I Lay Dying*." *ArQ*, XVI (1960), 26–38.

10 ROSCOE, Lavon. "An Interview With William Faulkner." *WR*, XV (1951), 300–304.

11 RUBIN, Louis D., Jr. "Chronicles of Yoknapatawpha: The Dynasties of William Faulkner." See 7.2.

12 SANDEEN, Ernest. "William Faulkner: Tragedian of Yoknapatawpha." See 13.4.

13 SARTRE, Jean-Paul. "On *The Sound and the Fury:* Time in the Work of Faulkner." *Literary and Philosophical Essays*. Trans. by Annette Michelson. London: Rider and Co., 1955, 79–87. Also in 39.18. [05360-Collr]

14 SCHWARTZ, Delmore. "The Fiction of William Faulkner." *SoR*, VII (1941), 145–160.

15 SCOTT, Arthur L. "The Myriad Perspectives of *Absalom, Absalom!*" *AQ*, VI (1954), 210–220.

16 SEIDEN, Melvin. "Faulkner's Ambiguous Negro." *MR*, IV (1963), 675–690.

17 SEWELL, Richard. "*Absalom, Absalom!*" *The Vision of Tragedy*. New Haven, Conn.: Yale Univ. Press, 1959, 133–147.

18 SIMON, John K. "The Scene and the Imagery of Metamorphosis in *As I Lay Dying*." *Criticism*, VII (1965), 1–22.

19 SIMPSON, Lewis P. "Isaac McCaslin and Temple Drake: The Fall of the New World Man." *Nine Essays in Modern Literature*. Ed. by Donald E. Stanford. Baton Rouge, La.: Louisiana State Univ. Press, 1965, 88–106.

20 SLABEY, Robert M. "Myth and Ritual in *Light in August*." *TSLL*, II (1960), 328–349.

21 SLATOFF, Walter J. "The Edge of Order: The Pattern of Faulkner's Rhetoric." *TCL*, III (1957), 107–127.

1 SOWDER, William J. "Colonel Thomas Sutpen as Existentialist Hero." *AL*, XXXIII (1962), 485–499.

2 SOWDER, William J. "Faulkner and Existentialism: A Note on the Generalissimo." *WSCL*, IV (1963), 163–171.

3 SOWDER, William J. "Lucas Beauchamp as Existential Hero." *CE*, XXV (1963), 115–127.

4 STALLMAN, R. W. "A Cryptogram: *As I Lay Dying.*" See 14.6.

5 STEIN, Jean. "William Faulkner." See 13.3. [A *Paris Review* Interview.]

6 STEWART, David H. "*Absalom* Reconsidered." *UTQ*, XXX (1960), 31–44.

7 STEWART, David H. "The Purpose of Faulkner's Ike." *Criticism*, III (1961), 333–342. [On Isaac McCaslin.]

8 STEWART, George R. and Joseph M. BACKUS. " 'Each in Its Ordered Place': Structure and Narrative in 'Benjy's Section' of *The Sound and the Fury.*" *AL*, XXIX (1958), 440–456.

9 SULLIVAN, Walter. "The Tragic Design of *Absalom, Absalom!*" *SAQ*, L (1951), 552–566.

10 SULTAN, Stanley. "Call Me Ishmael: The Hagiography of Isaac McCaslin." *TSLL*, III, i (1961), 50–66.

11 SWIGGART, Peter. "Moral and Temporal Order in *The Sound and the Fury.*" *SR*, LXI (1953), 221–237.

12 SWIGGART, Peter. "The Snopes Trilogy." *SR*, LXVIII (1960), 319–325. Also in 13.9.

13 SWIGGART, Peter. "Time in Faulkner's Novels." *MFS*, I (1955), 25–29.

14 TAYLOR, Walter F., Jr. "Let My People Go: The White Man's Heritage in *Go Down, Moses.*" *SAQ*, LVIII (1959), 20–32.

15 THOMPSON, Lawrance. "Mirror Analogues in *The Sound and the Fury.*" *EIE* (1952), 83–106. Also in 14.11 and 39.18.

16 TORCHIANA, Donald T. "Faulkner's *Pylon* and the Structure of Modernity." *MFS*, III (1957), 291–308.

17 TRITSCHLER, Donald. "The Unity of Faulkner's Shaping Vision." *MFS*, V (1959), 337–343.

18 TUCK, Dorothy. "*Light in August:* The Inwardness of the Understanding." *Approaches to the Twentieth-Century Novel*. Ed. by John Unterecker. New York: Crowell, 1965, 79–107.

19 TURNER, Arlin. "William Faulkner, Southern Novelist." *MissQ*, XIV (1961), 117–130.

20 VICKERY, Olga W. "*As I Lay Dying.*" *Perspective*, III (1950), 179–191.

21 VICKERY, Olga W. "Faulkner and the Contours of Time." *GaR*, XII (1958), 192–201.

22 VICKERY, Olga W. "Faulkner's First Novel." *WHR*, XI (1957), 251–256.

1 VICKERY, Olga W. "The Making of a Myth: *Sartoris.*" *WR*, XXII (1958), 209–219.

2 VICKERY, Olga W. "*The Sound and the Fury:* A Study in Perspective." *PMLA*, LXIX (1954), 1017–1037.

3 VICKERY, Olga W. "William Faulkner and the Figure in the Carpet." *SAQ*, LXIII (1964), 318–335.

4 WAGGONER, Hyatt H. "William Faulkner's Passion Week of the Heart." *The Tragic Vision and the Christian Faith.* Ed. by Nathan A. Scott, Jr. New York: Association Press, 1957, 306–323.

5 WARREN, Robert Penn. "Cowley's Faulkner." *NR*, LXV (Aug. 12, 1946), 176–180; (Aug. 26, 1946), 234–237. Also in 13.15 and 14.15.

6 WARREN, Robert Penn. "Faulkner: The South and the Negro." *SoR*, I (1965), 501–529. Also in 39.18.

7 WARREN, Robert Penn. "Introduction: Faulkner: Past and Future." See 39.18. [A survey of Faulkner criticism.]

8 WARREN, Robert Penn. "The Snopes World." *KR*, III (1941), 253–257.

9 WARREN, Robert Penn. "William Faulkner." *RLM*, nos. 40–42 (1959), 205–230.

10 WASIOLEK, Edward. "*As I Lay Dying:* Distortion in the Slow Eddy of Current Opinion." *Crit*, III (1959), 15–23.

11 WATKINS, Floyd C. "William Faulkner, The Individual and the World." *GaR*, XIV (1960), 238–247.

12 WATKINS, Floyd C. and Thomas Daniel YOUNG. "Revisions of Style in Faulkner's *The Hamlet.*" *MFS*, V (1959), 327–336.

13 WHAN, Edgar. "*Absalom, Absalom!* as Gothic Myth." *Perspective*, III (1950), 192–201.

14 WHEELER, Otis B. "Faulkner's Wilderness." *AL*, XXXI (1959), 127–136.

15 WHEELER, Otis B. "Some Uses of Folk Humor by Faulkner." *MissQ*, XVII (1964), 107–122.

16 WHITBREAD, Thomas. "The Snopes Trilogy: The Setting of *The Mansion.*" See 14.8.

17 WILLIAMS, Aubrey. "William Faulkner's 'Temple' of Innocence." *RIP*, XLVII (1960), 51–67.

18 WYNNE, Carolyn. "Aspects of Space: John Marin and William Faulkner." *AQ*, XVI (1964), 59–71.

19 ZINK, Karl E. "Faulkner's Garden: Woman and the Immemorial Earth." *MFS*, II (1956), 139–149.

20 ZINK, Karl E. "Flux and the Frozen Moment: The Imagery of Stasis in Faulkner's Prose." *PMLA*, LXXI (1956), 285–301.

21 ZINK, Karl E. "William Faulkner: Form as Experience." *SAQ*, LIII (1954), 384–403. [A study of Faulkner's style.]

22 ZOELLNER, Robert H. "Faulkner's Prose Style in *Absalom, Absalom!*" *AL*, XXX (1959), 486–502.

Fitzgerald, F. Scott (1896–1940)

TEXTS

1 *The Crack-up; with Other Uncollected Pieces, Notebooks, and Unpublished Letters.* Ed. by Edmund Wilson. New York: New Directions, 1956.

2 KUEHL, John, ed. *The Apprentice Fiction of F. Scott Fitzgerald, 1909–1917.* With introd. New Brunswick, N.J.: Rutgers Univ. Press, 1965.

3 KUEHL, John R. "Scott Fitzgerald's 'Thoughtbook'." *PULC*, XXVI (1965), 102–108. Repr. as *The Thoughtbook of Francis Scott Key Fitzgerald.* Princeton, N.J.: Princeton Univ. Library, 1965. [Fitzgerald's 1910–1911 diary.]

4 MIZENER, Arthur, ed. *Afternoon of an Author; A Selection of Uncollected Stories and Essays.* With introd. Princeton, N.J.: Princeton Univ. Library, 1957.

5 PIPER, Henry Dan. "Scott Fitzgerald's Prep-School Writings: Several Newly Discovered Additions to the Canon of His Published Works." *PULC*, XVII (1955), 1–10.

BIBLIOGRAPHY

6 BEEBE, Maurice and Jackson R. BRYER. "Criticism of F. Scott Fitzgerald: A Selected Checklist." *MFS*, VII (1961), 82–94.

7 BRUCCOLI, Matthew J. The Composition of *"Tender is the Night": A Study of the Manuscripts.* Pittsburgh, Pa.: Univ. of Pittsburgh Press, 1963.

8 BRUCCOLI, Matthew J. "Material for a Centenary Edition of *Tender is the Night.*" *SB*, XVII (1964), 177–193.

9 BRYER, Jackson R. *The Critical Reputation of F. Scott Fitzgerald: A Bibliographical Study.* Hamden, Conn.: Shoe String Press, 1967.

10 BRYER, Jackson R. "F. Scott Fitzgerald: A Review of Research and Scholarship." *TSLL*, V (1963), 147–163.

11 MIZENER, Arthur. "The F. Scott Fitzgerald Papers." *PULC*, XII (1951), 190–195.

BIOGRAPHICAL AND CRITICAL BOOKS

12 CROSS, K. G. W. *F. Scott Fitzgerald.* New York: Grove Press, 1964.

13 EBLE, Kenneth. *F. Scott Fitzgerald.* New York: Twayne, 1963. [T-36-C&UPS]

14 GOLDHURST, William. *F. Scott Fitzgerald and His Contemporaries.* Cleveland, Ohio: World Publishing, 1963.

15 GRAHAM, Sheilah and Gerold FRANK. *Beloved Infidel: The Education of a Woman.* New York: Holt, 1958. [Devoted in part to the relationship between Miss Graham and Fitzgerald.] [S-3457-Ban]

16 GRAHAM, Sheilah. *College of One.* New York: Viking, 1967.

17 GRAHAM, Sheilah. *The Rest of the Story.* New York: Coward-McCann, 1964. [H2951-Ban]

1   KAZIN, Alfred, ed. *F. Scott Fitzgerald: The Man and His Work*. Cleveland, Ohio: World Publishing, 1951. [Essays by various hands.] [00410-Collr]

2   LEHAN, Richard D. *F. Scott Fitzgerald and the Craft of Fiction*. Carbondale and Edwardsville, Ill.: Southern Illinois Univ. Press, 1966.

3   MILLER, James E., Jr. *F. Scott Fitzgerald: His Art and His Technique*. New York: New York Univ. Press, 1964 (Orig.). [An expansion of Miller's earlier (1957) *The Fictional Technique of Scott Fitzgerald*.] [NYU]

4   MIZENER, Arthur. *The Far Side of Paradise: A Biography of F. Scott Fitzgerald*. 2nd rev. ed. Boston: Houghton Mifflin, 1965. [46-SenEd]

5   MIZENER, Arthur, ed. *F. Scott Fitzgerald: A Collection of Critical Essays*. Englewood Cliffs, N.J.: Prentice-Hall, 1963. [By various hands.] [S-TC-27-Spec]

6   PEROSA, Sergio. *The Art of F. Scott Fitzgerald*. Ann Arbor, Mich.: Univ. of Michigan Press, 1965.

7   PIPER, Henry Dan. *F. Scott Fitzgerald, A Critical Portrait*. New York: Holt, Rinehart & Winston, 1965.

8   SHAIN, Charles E. *F. Scott Fitzgerald*. UMPAW, No. 15. Minneapolis, Minn.: Univ. of Minnesota Press, 1961. [UMP]

9   SKLAR, Robert. *F. Scott Fitzgerald: The Last Laocoön*. New York: Oxford Univ. Press, 1967.

10 TURNBULL, Andrew, ed. *The Letters of F. Scott Fitzgerald*. New York: Scribner, 1963.

11 TURNBULL, Andrew. *Scott Fitzgerald*. New York: Scribner, 1962. [Biography.] [SL-95-Scrib]

12 TURNBULL, Andrew, ed. *Scott Fitzgerald: Letters to His Daughter*. Introd. by Frances Fitzgerald Lanahan. New York: Scribner, 1965.

BIOGRAPHICAL AND CRITICAL ESSAYS

13 ALDRIDGE, John W. "Fitzgerald—The Horror and the Vision of Paradise." See 5.1 and 50.5.

14 ALDRIDGE, John W. "The Life of Gatsby." See 14.5.

15 BABB, Howard S. "*The Great Gatsby* and the Grotesque." *Criticism*, V (1963), 336–348.

16 BALDWIN, Charles C. "F. Scott Fitzgerald." See 5.3.

17 BARRETT, William. "Fitzgerald and America." *PR*, XVIII (1951), 345–353.

18 BERRYMAN, John. "F. Scott Fitzgerald." *KR*, VIII (1946) 103–112.

19 BEWLEY, Marius. "Scott Fitzgerald's Criticism of America." *SR*, LXII (1954), 223–246. Repr. in 50.5. [On *The Great Gatsby*.]

20 BEWLEY, Marius. "Scott Fitzgerald and the Collapse of the American Dream." *The Eccentric Design: Form in the Classic American Novel*. New York: Columbia Univ. Press, 1959, 259–287. [Col]

21 BEZANSON, Walter. "Scott Fitzgerald: Bedevilled Prince Charming." See 13.1.

1 BICKNELL, John W. "The Waste Land of Scott Fitzgerald." *VQR*, XXX (1954), 556–572. [Questions the validity of Fitzgerald's tragic vision.]

2 BISHOP, John Peale. "The Missing All." *VQR*, XIII (1937), 106–121. Repr. in *The Collected Essays of John Peale Bishop*. Ed. by Edmund Wilson. New York: Scribner, 1948, 66–77. [Fitzgerald and Hemingway.]

3 BRUCCOLI, Matthew J. "*Tender Is The Night* and the Reviewers." *MFS*, VII (1961), 49–54.

4 BURNAM, Tom. "The Eyes of Dr. Eckleburg: A Re-examination of *The Great Gatsby*." *CE*, XIV (1952), 7–12. Repr. in 50.5.

5 CARDWELL, Guy A. "The Lyric World of Scott Fitzgerald." *VQR*, XXXVIII (1962), 299–323.

6 CARLISLE, E. Fred. "The Triple Vision of Nick Carraway." *MFS*, XI (1966), 351–360.

7 CHASE, Richard. See 4.8.

8 COWLEY, Malcolm. "Introduction." *The Stories of F. Scott Fitzgerald*. New York: Scribner, 1951, vii–xxv.

9 COWLEY, Malcolm. "F. Scott Fitzgerald: The Romance of Money." *WR*, XVII (1953), 245–255.

10 COWLEY, Malcolm. "Third Act and Epilogue." See 50.1 and 50.5. [Fitzgerald's last years.]

11 DOS PASSOS, John. "A Note on Fitzgerald." See 49.1 and 50.1.

12 DOYNO, Victor A. "Patterns in *The Great Gatsby*." *MFS*. XII (1966), 415–426.

13 DYSON, A. E. "*The Great Gatsby:* Thirty-Six Years After." *MFS*, VII (1961), 37–48. Repr. in 50.5.

14 EBLE, Kenneth. "The Craft of Revision: *The Great Gatsby*." *AL*, XXXVI (1964), 315–326.

15 EMBLER, Weller. "F. Scott Fitzgerald and the Future." See 50.1.

16 FIEDLER, Leslie. "Some Notes on F. Scott Fitzgerald." *An End to Innocence*. Boston: Beacon Press, 1955, 174–182. Repr. in 50.5.

17 FRASER, John. "Dust and Dreams in *The Great Gatsby*." *ELH*, XXXII (1965), 554–564.

18 FRIEDMAN, Norman. "Versions of Form in Fiction: *Great Expectations* and *The Great Gatsby*." *Accent*, XIV (1954), 246–264.

19 FRIEDRICH, Otto. "F. Scott Fitzgerald: Money, Money, Money." *ASch*, XXIX (1960), 392–405.

20 FROHOCK, W. M. "Morals, Manners, and Scott Fitzgerald." *SWR*, XL (1955), 220–228. Repr. in Frohock, *Strangers to this Ground*. Dallas, Tex.: Southern Methodist Univ. Press, 1961, 36–62.

21 FUSSELL, Edwin S. "Fitzgerald's Brave New World." *ELH*, XIX (1952), 291–306.

22 GEISMAR, Maxwell. "F. Scott Fitzgerald: Orestes at the Ritz." See 5.17.

1 GILES, Barbara. "The Dream of F. Scott Fitzgerald." *Mainstream*, X (March, 1957), 1–12.

2 HALL, William F. "Dialogue and Theme in *Tender Is the Night*." *MLN*, LXXVI (1961), 616–622.

3 HANZO, Thomas A. "The Theme and the Narrator of *The Great Gatsby*." *MFS*, II (1956), 183–190.

4 HART, John E. "Fitzgerald's *The Last Tycoon:* A Search for Identity." *MFS*, VII (1961), 63–70.

5 HARVEY, W. J. "Theme and Texture in *The Great Gatsby*." *ES*, XXXVIII (1957), 12–20.

6 HINDUS, Milton. "The Mysterious Eyes of Doctor T. J. Eckleburg." *BUSE*, III (1957), 22–31.

7 HOFFMAN, Frederick J. "Fitzgerald's *The Great Gatsby*." See 6.10.

8 HOFFMAN, Frederick J. "Points of Moral Reference: A Comparative Study of Edith Wharton and F. Scott Fitzgerald." *EIE*, 1949. New York: Columbia Univ. Press, 1950, 147–176.

9 HOLMES, Charles S. "Fitzgerald: The American Theme." *PS*, VI (1952), 243–252.

10 HUGHES, Riley. "F. Scott Fitzgerald: The Touch of Disaster." See 13.4.

11 KALLICH, Martin. "F. Scott Fitzgerald: Money or Morals." *UKCR*, XV (1949), 271–280.

12 KAZIN, Alfred. "Fitzgerald: An American Confession." *QRL*, II (1946), 341–346. Also in 50.1.

13 KAZIN, Alfred. "Into the Thirties: All the Lost Generations." See 2.12.

14 KREUTER, Kent and Gretchen. "The Moralism of the Later Fitzgerald." *MFS*, VII (1961), 71–81.

15 KUEHL, John. "Scott Fitzgerald's Critical Opinions." *MFS*, VII (1961), 3–18.

16 KUEHL, John. "Scott Fitzgerald's Reading." *PULC*, XXII (1961), 58–89.

17 KUEHL, John. "Scott Fitzgerald: Romantic and Realist." *TSLL*, I (1959), 412–426.

18 LAUTER, Paul. "Plato's Stepchildren, Gatsby and Cohn." *MFS*, IX (1963), 338–346.

19 LEIGHTON, Lawrence. "An Autopsy and a Prescription." *H&H*, V (1932), 519–540.

21 LIGHT, James F. "Political Conscience in the Novels of F. Scott Fitzgerald," *BSTCF*, IV, i (1963), 13–25.

22 LUBELL, Albert J. "The Fitzgerald Revival." *SAQ*, LIV (1955), 95–106.

23 LUCAS, John. "In Praise of Scott Fitzgerald." *CritQ*, V (1963), 132–147.

1 MAC KENDRICK, Paul L. "The Great Gatsby and Trimalchio." *CJ*, XLV (1950), 307–314.

2 MAURER, Robert E. "F. Scott Fitzgerald's Unfinished Novel, *The Last Tycoon*." *BuUS*, III (1952), 139–156.

3 MC DONNELL, Robert F. "Eggs and Eyes in *The Great Gatsby. MFS*, VII (1961), 32–36.

4 MIZENER, Arthur. "F. Scott Fitzgerald, *The Great Gatsby*." See 14.7.

5 MIZENER, Arthur. "F. Scott Fitzgerald (1896–1940): The Poet of Borrowed Time." *Lives of Eighteen from Princeton*. Ed. by Willard Thorp. Princeton, N.J.: Princeton Univ. Press, 1946. Repr. in 50.1.

6 MIZENER, Arthur. "Scott Fitzgerald and the Imaginative Possession of American Life." *SR*, LIV (1946), 66–86. Also in 12.14 and 50.1.

7 MIZENER, Arthur. "Fitzgerald in the Twenties." *PR*, XVII (1950), 7–38.

8 MIZENER, Arthur. "The Maturity of Scott Fitzgerald." *SR*, LXVII (1959), 658–675. Also in 13.9 and 50.5.

9 MIZENER, Arthur. "The Novel of Manners in America." *KR*, XII (1950), 1–19.

10 MIZENER, Arthur. "The Voice of Scott Fitzgerald's Prose." *E&S*, XVI (1963), 56–67.

11 MORRIS, Wright. "Fitzgerald: The Function of Nostalgia." See 13.14. and 50.5.

12 O'HARA, John. "Introduction." *The Portable F. Scott Fitzgerald*. New York: Viking, 1945. vii–xix.

13 PIPER, Henry Dan. "Fitzgerald's Cult of Disillusion." *AQ*, II (1951), 69–80.

14 PIPER, Henry Dan. "Frank Norris and Scott Fitzgerald." *HLQ*, XIX (1956), 393–400.

15 PIPER, Henry Dan. "The Lost Decade." *Interim*, II (1945), 39–44.

16 RALEIGH, John Henry. "F. Scott Fitzgerald's *The Great Gatsby:* Legendary Bases and Allegorical Significances." *UKCR*, XXIII (1957), 283–291; XXIV (1957), 55–58. Repr. in 50.5.

17 RIDDEL, Joseph N. "F. Scott Fitzgerald, the Jamesian Inheritance, and the Morality of Fiction." *MFS*, XI (1966), 331–350.

18 ROBBINS, J. Albert. "Fitzgerald and the Simple, Inarticulate Farmer." *MFS*, VII (1961), 365–368.

19 ROSENFELD, Paul. "F. Scott Fitzgerald." *Men Seen*. New York: Dial Press, 1925, 215–224. Also in 49.1 and 50.1.

20 ROSS, Alan. "Rumble Among the Drums—F. Scott Fitzgerald (1896–1940) and the Jazz Age." *Horizon*, XVIII (1948), 420–435.

21 SAMUELS, Charles Thomas. "The Greatness of *Gatsby*." *MR*, VII (1966), 783–794.

22 SAVAGE, D. S. "The Significance of F. Scott Fitzgerald." *ArQ*, VIII (1952), 197–210. Repr. in 50.5.

1 SCHOENWALD, Richard L. "F. Scott Fitzgerald as John Keats." *BUSE*, III (1957), 12–21.

2 SCHULBERG, Budd. "Old Scott: The Mask, the Myth, and the Man." *Esquire*, LV (1961), 97–101.

3 SCRIMGEOUR, Gary J. "Against *The Great Gatsby.*" *Criticism*, VIII (1966), 75–86. [Comparison with Conrad's "Heart of Darkness."]

4 SPENCER, Benjamin T. "Fitzgerald and the American Ambivalence." *SAQ*, LXVI (1967), 367.

5 STALLMAN, Robert W. "By the Dawn's Early Light *Tender Is the Night.*" See 14.6.

6 STALLMAN, Robert W. "Conrad and *The Great Gatsby.*" *TCL*, I (1955), 5–12. Also in 14.6.

7 STALLMAN, Robert W. "Gatsby and the Hole in Time." *MFS*, I (Nov., 1955), 2–16. Repr. in 14.6.

8 STANTON, Robert. " 'Daddy's Girl': Symbol and Theme in *Tender is the Night.*" *MFS*, IV (1958), 136–142.

9 TANSELLE, G. Thomas and Jackson R. BRYER. "*The Great Gatsby:* A Study in Literary Reputation." *NMQ*, XXXIII (1964), 409–425.

10 TAYLOR, Douglas. "*The Great Gatsby:* Style and Myth." *UKCR*, XX (1953), 30–40. Also in 14.11.

11 TRILLING, Lionel. "Introduction." *The Great Gatsby*. New York: New Directions, 1945, vii–xiv.

12 TROY, William. "Scott Fitzgerald: The Authority of Failure." *Accent*, VI (1945), 56–60. Also in 13.9, 13.15, and 50.1.

13 WANNING, Andrews. "Fitzgerald and His Brethren." *PR*, XII (1945), 545–551. Also in 50.1.

14 WEIMER, David R. "Lost City: F. Scott Fitzgerald." *The City as Metaphor*. New York: Random House, 1966, 88–103.

15 WEIR, Charles, Jr. " 'An Invite with Gilded Edges'." *VQR*, XX (1944), 100–113. Also in 50.1.

16 WESCOTT, Glenway. "The Moral of F. Scott Fitzgerald." See 49.1 and 50.1.

17 WHITE, Eugene. "The 'Intricate Destiny' of Dick Diver." *MFS*, VII (1961), 55–62.

18 WILSON, Edmund. "The Delegate from Great Neck." See 14.14 and 50.1.

19 WILSON, Edmund. "A Weekend at Ellerslie." See 14.14. [Reminiscences of a weekend with Fitzgerald in 1928.]

20 WILSON, Robert N. "Fitzgerald as Icarus." *AR*, XVII (1957), 481–492.

21 YATES, Donald A. "The Road to 'Paradise': Fitzgerald's Literary Apprenticeship." *MFS*, VII (1961), 19–32.

55

Hawkes, John (1925–)

BIBLIOGRAPHY

1 BRYER, Jackson R. "John Hawkes." *Crit*, VI, ii (1963), 89–94.

BIOGRAPHICAL AND CRITICAL ESSAYS

2 EDENBAUM, Robert I. "John Hawkes: *The Lime Twig* and Tenuous Horrors." *MR*, VII (1966), 462–475.

3 ENCK, John. "John Hawkes: An Interview." *WSCL*, VI (1965), 141–155.

4 FIEDLER, Leslie. "A Lonely American Eccentric: The Pleasures of John Hawkes." *NewL*, XLIII (Dec. 12, 1960), 12–14. Repr. as introd. to Hawkes, *The Lime Twig*. Norfolk, Conn.: New Directions, 1961, vii–xiv.

5 FROHOCK, W. M. "John Hawkes's Vision of Violence." *SWR*, L (1965), 69–79.

6 GUERARD, Albert J. "The Prose Style of John Hawkes." *Crit*, V, ii (1963), 19–29.

7 HAWKES, John. "John Hawkes on His Novels." *MR*, VII (1966), 449–461.

8 MALIN, Irving. See 11.3.

9 MATTHEWS, Charles. "The Destructive Vision of John Hawkes." *Crit*, VI, ii (1963), 38–52.

10 OBERBECK, S. K. "John Hawkes: The Smile Slashed by a Razor." See 13.12.

11 RATNER, Marc. "The Constructed Vision: The Fiction of John Hawkes." *SA*, XI (1965), 345–357.

12 REUTLINGER, D. P. "*The Cannibal:* 'The Reality of Victim'." *Crit*, VI, ii (1963), 30–37.

13 ROVIT, Earl. "The Fiction of John Hawkes: An Introductory View." *MFS*, XI (1964), 150–162.

14 TRACHTENBERG, Alan. "Barth and Hawkes: Two Fabulists." *Crit*, VI, ii (1963), 4–18.

Hemingway, Ernest (1899–1961)

TEXTS

15 *A Farewell to Arms*. Introd. by Robert Penn Warren. New York: Scribner, 1949. [SL-61-Scrib]

16 COWLEY, Malcolm, ed. *The Portable Hemingway*. New York: Viking, 1945.

1   POORE, Charles, ed. *The Hemingway Reader*. New York: Scribner, 1953.

2   WHITE, William, ed. *By-Line: Ernest Hemingway*. New York: Scribner, 1967. [Hemingway's journalism.]

BIBLIOGRAPHY

3   BEEBE, Maurice. "Criticism of Ernest Hemingway: A Selected Checklist with an Index to Studies of Separate Works." *MFS*, I (Aug., 1955), 36–45. Repr., with additions, in 56.11.

4   HANNEMAN, Audre. *Ernest Hemingway: A Comprehensive Bibliography*. Princeton, N.J.: Princeton Univ. Press, 1967.

5   MERIWETHER, James B. "The Text of Ernest Hemingway." *PBSA*, LVII (1963), 403–421. [Discusses need for and problems in an edition of Hemingway.]

6   SAMUELS, Lee. *A Hemingway Check List*. New York: Scribner, 1951.

7   STEPHENS, Robert O. "Some Additions to the Hemingway Checklist." *ABC*, XVII, viii (1967), 9–11.

BIOGRAPHICAL AND CRITICAL BOOKS

8   ASSELINEAU, Roger, ed. *The Literary Reputation of Hemingway in Europe*. Introd. by Heinrich Straumann. New York: New York Univ. Press, 1965 (Orig.). [Essays by various hands.] [NYU]

9   ATKINS, John. *The Art of Ernest Hemingway*. London: Peter Nevill, 1952.

10   BAKER, Carlos, ed. *Ernest Hemingway: Critiques of Four Major Novels*. New York: Scribner, 1962. [Reprints essays by various hands.] [Scrib]

11   BAKER, Carlos, ed. *Hemingway and His Critics: An International Anthology*. American Century Series. New York: Hill & Wang, 1961. [Essays by various hands; includes useful checklist of Hemingway criticism.] [AC-36-Am Cen]

12   BAKER, Carlos. *Hemingway: The Writer as Artist*. Princeton, N.J.: Princeton Univ. Press, 1964. [Third, revised edition, with new chapter on Hemingway's last decade.]

13   BAKER, Sheridan. *Ernest Hemingway: An Introduction and Interpretation*. New York: Holt, Rinehart & Winston, 1967.

14   CALLAGHAN, Morley. *That Summer in Paris: Memories of Tangled Friendships with Hemingway, Fitzgerald, and Some Others*. New York: Coward-McCann, 1963. [8664-LE-Dell]

15   DE FALCO, Joseph. *The Hero in Hemingway's Short Stories*. Pittsburgh Pa.: Univ. of Pittsburgh Press, 1963 (Orig.). [Pitts]

16   FENTON, Charles A. *The Apprenticeship of Ernest Hemingway: The Early Years*. New York: Viking, 1954. [MP-385-Ment]

17   Hanrahan, Gene Z., ed. *The Wild Years*. New York: Dell, 1962. [Selections from Hemingway's Toronto *Star* articles, 1920–1924.]

18   HEMINGWAY, Leicester. *My Brother, Ernest Hemingway*. Cleveland, Ohio: World Publishing, 1962. [T344-Prem]

1 HOTCHNER, A. E. *Papa Hemingway: A Personal Memoir.* New York: Random House, 1966. [Q3366-Ben]

2 KILEY, John G. *Hemingway: An Old Friend Remembers.* New York: Hawthorn, 1965.

3 KILLINGER, John. *Hemingway and the Dead Gods: A Study in Existentialism.* Lexington, Ky.: Univ. of Kentucky Press, 1960. [C-191-Ctdl]

4 LEWIS, Robert W., Jr. *Hemingway on Love.* Austin, Tex.: Univ. of Texas Press, 1965.

5 LOEB, Harold. *The Way It Was.* New York: Criterion Books, 1959. [Loeb, the prototype of Robert Cohn in *The Sun Also Rises*, gives his version of the characters and events in that novel.]

6 MC CAFFERY, John K. M., ed. *Ernest Hemingway: The Man and His Work.* Cleveland Ohio: World Publishing, 1950. [Essays by various hands.]

7 MONTGOMERY, Constance C. *Hemingway in Michigan.* New York: Fleet, 1966. [Of limited interest, but includes three unpublished stories written in high school.]

8 ROSS, Lillian. *Portrait of Hemingway.* New York: Simon and Schuster, 1961. [Appeared originally as a Profile, *NY*, May 13, 1950.] [SS3-Avon]

9 ROVIT, Earl. *Ernest Hemingway.* New York: Twayne, 1963. [T-41-C&UPS]

10 SANDERSON, S. F. *Ernest Hemingway.* Edinburgh: Oliver & Boyd; New York: Grove Press, 1961.

11 SANFORD, Marcelline Hemingway. *At the Hemingways: A Family Portrait.* Boston: Atlantic, Little Brown, 1962.

12 SCOTT, Nathan A., Jr. *Ernest Hemingway: A Critical Essay.* CWCP. Grand Rapids, Mich.: Eerdmans, 1966.

13 WEEKS, Robert P., ed. *Hemingway: A Collection of Critical Essays.* Englewood Cliffs, N.J.: Prentice-Hall, 1962. [S-TC-8-Spec]

14 YOUNG, Philip. *Ernest Hemingway.* UMPAW, No. 1. Minneapolis, Minn.: Univ. of Minnesota Press, 1959. [UMP]

15 YOUNG, Philip. *Ernest Hemingway: A Reconsideration.* University Park, Pa.: Penn. State Univ. Press, 1966.

BIOGRAPHICAL AND CRITICAL ESSAYS

16 ADAMS, Richard P. "Sunrise Out of the Waste Land." *TSE*, IX (1959), 119–131. [Eliot's influence on *The Sun Also Rises*.]

17 ALDRIDGE, John W. "Hemingway and Europe." *Shenandoah*, XII (1961), 11–24.

18 ALDRIDGE, John W. "Hemingway: The Etiquette of the Berserk." *Mandrake*, II (1954), 331–341. Repr. in 12.15.

19 ANDERSON, Charles R. "Hemingway's Other Style." *MLN*, LXXVI (1961), 434–442. Also in 56.10.

1 BACKMAN, Melvin. "Hemingway: The Matador and the Crucified." *MFS*, I (Aug. 1955), 2–11. Also in 13.9, 56.10, and 56.11.

2 BAKER, Carlos. "Citizen of the World." See 56.11.

3 BAKER, Carlos. "Ernest Hemingway, *A Farewell to Arms.*" See 14.7.

4 BAKER, Carlos. "Hemingway's Wastelanders." *VQR*, XXVIII (1952), 373–392.

5 BAKER, Carlos. "Letters from Hemingway." *PULC*, XXIV (1963), 101–107.

6 BAKER, Carlos. "The Mountain and the Plain." *VQR*, XXVII (1951), 410–418. [Imagery in *A Farewell to Arms.*]

7 BARDACKE, Theodore. "Hemingway's Women." See 57.6.

8 BAREA, Arturo. "Not Spain But Hemingway." *Horizon*, III (1941), 350–361. Also in 56.11. [on *For Whom the Bell Tolls.*]

9 BARNES, Lois L. "The Helpless Hero of Ernest Hemingway." *S&S*, XVII (1953), 1–25.

10 BEACH, Joseph Warren. "Ernest Hemingway: Empirical Ethics" and "Ernest Hemingway: The Esthetics of Simplicity." See 5.5.

11 BEACH, Joseph Warren. "How Do You Like It Now, Gentlemen?" *SR*, LIX (1951), 311–328. Also in 56.11. [Hemingway's major themes.]

12 BESSIE, Alvah. "Hemingway's *For Whom the Bell Tolls.*" *NewM*, XXXVII (Nov. 25, 1940), 25–29. Also in 56.10.

13 BICKFORD, Sylvester. "Hemingway's Extended Vision: *The Old Man and the Sea.*" *PMLA*, LXXXI (1966), 130–138.

14 BISHOP, John Peale. "Homage to Hemingway." See 13.2.

15 BISHOP, John Peale. "The Missing All." *VQR*, XIII (1937), 106–121. Repr. in 57.6. [On Fitzgerald and Hemingway.]

16 BROWN, Deming. "Hemingway in Russia." *AQ*, V (1953), 143–156. Also in 56.11.

17 BURGUM, Edwin Berry. "Ernest Hemingway and the Psychology of the Lost Generation." See 8.4.

18 BURHANS, Clinton S., Jr. "*The Old Man and the Sea:* Hemingway's Tragic Vision of Man." *AL*, XXXI (1960), 446–455. Also in 14.11, 56.10, and 56.11.

19 BURNAM, Tom. "Primitivism and Masculinity in the Work of Ernest Hemingway." *MFS*, I (Aug., 1955), 20–24.

20 CARGILL, Oscar. See 2.7.

21 CARPENTER, Frederic I. "Hemingway Achieves the Fifth Dimension." *PMLA*, LXIX (1954), 711–718. Also in 56.11.

22 CLENDENNING, John. "Hemingway's Gods, Dead and Alive." *TSLL*, III (1962), 489–502.

23 COLVERT, James B. "Ernest Hemingway's Morality in Action." *AL*, XXVII (1955), 372–385.

24 CORIN, Fernand. "Steinbeck and Hemingway—A Study in Literary Economy." *RLV*, XXIV (1958), 60–75, 153–163.

1 COWLEY, Malcolm. "Hemingway and the Hero." *NewR*, CI (Dec. 4, 1944), 754–758.

2 COWLEY, Malcolm. "Hemingway at Midnight." *NewR*, CXI (Aug. 14, 1944), 190–195.

3 COWLEY, Malcolm. "Nightmare and Ritual in Hemingway." See 57.13. [Introduction to *The Portable Hemingway*.]

4 D'AGOSTINO, Nemi. "The Later Hemingway." *SR*, LXVIII (1960), 482–493. Repr. in 57.13.

5 DAICHES, David. "Ernest Hemingway." *CE*, II (1941), 725–736.

6 DANIEL, Robert. "Hemingway and His Heroes." *QQ*, LIV (1947), 471–485.

7 DAWSON, William Forrest. "Ernest Hemingway: Petoskey Interview." *MAQR*, LXIV (1958), 114–123. [Background for the early Michigan stories.]

8 DRINNON, Richard. "In the American Heartland: Hemingway and Death." *PsyR*, LII (1965), 5–31.

9 EASTMAN, Max. "Bull in the Afternoon." *NewR*, LXXV (June 7, 1933), 94–97. Repr. in 57.6.

10 EVANS, Robert. "Hemingway and the Pale Cast of Thought." *AL*, XXXVIII (1966), 161–176.

11 FENIMORE, Edward. "English and Spanish in *For Whom the Bell Tolls*." See 57.6.

12 FLANAGAN, John T. "Hemingway's Debt to Sherwood Anderson." *JEGP*, LIV (1955), 507–520.

13 FRANKENBERG, Lloyd. "Themes and Characters in Hemingway's Latest Period." *SoR*, VII (1942), 776–788.

14 FREEDMAN, Richard. "Hemingway's Spanish War Dispatches." *TSLL*, I, ii (1959), 171–180.

15 FRIEDMAN, Norman. "Criticism and the Novel." *AR*, XVIII (1958), 343–370. Also in 14.11. [On misreadings of *A Farewell to Arms*.]

16 FRIEDRICH, Otto. "Ernest Hemingway: Joy Through Strength." *ASch*, XXVI (1957), 470, 518–530.

17 FROHOCK, W. M. "Ernest Hemingway: Violence and Discipline." *SWR*, XXXII (1947), 89–97, 184–193.

18 FUCHS, Daniel. "Ernest Hemingway: Literary Critic." *AL*, XXXVI (1965), 431–451.

19 FUSSELL, Edwin. "Hemingway and Mark Twain." *Accent*, XIV (1954), 199–206.

20 GEISMAR, Maxwell. "No Man Alone Now." *VQR*, XVII (1941), 517–534.

21 GERARD, Albert. "Ernest Hemingway." *RLV*, XXI (1955), 35–50.

22 GLASSER, William A. "*A Farewell to Arms*." *SR*, LXXIV (1966), 453–469.

23 GORDON, Caroline. "Notes on Hemingway and Kafka." *SR*, LVII (1949), 215–226.

1 GRAHAM, John. "Ernest Hemingway: The Meaning of Style." *MFS*, VI (1960), 298–313. Also in 56.10.

2 GURKO, Leo. "The Achievement of Ernest Hemingway." *CE*, XIII (1952), 368–375.

3 GURKO, Leo. "Hemingway in Spain." See 57.6.

4 GURKO, Leo. "*The Old Man and the Sea*." *CE*, XVII (1955), 11–15.

5 GUTTMANN, Allen. "Mechanized Doom: Ernest Hemingway and the Spanish Civil War." *MR*, I (1960), 541–561. Also in 56.11.

6 HALE, Nancy. "Hemingway and the Courage to Be." *VQR*, XXXVIII (1962), 620–639.

7 HALLIDAY, E. M. "Hemingway's Ambiguity: Symbolism and Irony." *AL*, XXVIII (1956), 1–22. Also in 56.10 and 57.13.

8 HALLIDAY, E. M. "Hemingway's Narrative Perspective." *SR*, LX (1952), 202–218. Also in 13.9 and 56.10.

9 HART, Robert C. "Hemingway on Writing." *CE*, XVIII (1957), 314–320.

10 HARTWICK, Harry. See 6.3.

11 HATCHER, Harlan. See 6.5.

12 HEMINGWAY, Ernest. "The Original Conclusion to *A Farewell to Arms*." See 56.10.

13 HEMPHILL, George. "Hemingway and James." *KR*, XI (1949), 50–60. Also in 57.6.

14 HOLMAN, C. Hugh. "Hemingway and Emerson." *MFS*, I (Aug., 1955), 12–16.

15 HOVEY, Richard B. "*The Torrents of Spring:* Prefigurations in the Early Hemingway." *CE*, XXVI (1965), 460–464.

16 JOHNSON, Edgar. "Farewell the Separate Peace." *SR*, XLVIII (1940), 289–300. Also in 57.6.

17 JONES, John A. "Hemingway: The Critics and the Public Legend." *WHR*, XIII (1959), 387–400.

18 KASHKEEN, Ivan. "Alive in the Midst of Death." *SovL*, No. 7 (1956), 160–172. Also in 56.11. [By Hemingway's Russian friend and correspondent.]

19 KASHKEEN, Ivan. "Ernest Hemingway: A Tragedy of Craftsmanship." *IntL*, V (1945), 76–108. Also in 57.6.

20 KAZIN, Alfred. "Into the Thirties: All the Lost Generations." See 2.12 and 57.6.

21 LAIR, Robert L. "Hemingway and Cézanne: An Indebtedness." *MFS*, VI (1960), 165–168.

22 LAUTER, Paul. "Plato's Stepchildren, Gatsby and Cohn." *MFS*, IX (1963), 338–346.

23 LEHAN, Richard. "Camus and Hemingway." *WSCL*, I (1960), 37–48.

24 LEIGHTON, Lawrence. "An Autopsy and a Prescription." *H&H*, V (1932), 519–539.

1 LEVIN, Harry. "Observations on the Style of Hemingway." *KR*, XIII (1951), 581–609. Also in 56.11 and 57.13.

2 LEWIS, Robert W., Jr. "Tristan or Jacob: The Choice of *The Sun Also Rises*." See 14.11.

3 LEWIS, Wyndham. "The Dumb Ox, a Study of Ernest Hemingway." *ARev*, VI (1934), 289–312. Also in Lewis, *Men Without Art*. London: Cassell & Co., 1934, 17–40. [On Hemingway's limitations.]

4 LID, Richard W. "Hemingway and the Need for Speech." *MFS*, VIII (1962), 401–407.

5 LIGHT, James F. "The Religion of Death in *A Farewell to Arms*." *MFS*, VII (1961), 169–173. Also in 56.10.

6 LISCA, Peter. "The Structure of Hemingway's *Across the River and into the Trees*." *MFS*, XII (1966), 232–250.

7 LOVETT, Robert Morss. "Ernest Hemingway." *EJ*, XXI (1932), 609–617.

8 MAUROIS, André. "Ernest Hemingway." See 56.11.

9 MC CORMICK, John. "Hemingway and History." *WR*, XVII (1953), 87–98. [Argues Hemingway's importance as social historian.]

10 MIZENER, Arthur. "The Two Hemingways." *The Great Experiment in American Literature: Six Lectures*. Ed. by Carl Bode. New York: Praeger, 1961, 135–151.

11 MOLONEY, Michael F. "Ernest Hemingway: The Missing Third Dimension." See 13.4 and 56.11.

12 MOORE, Geoffrey. "*The Sun Also Rises:* Notes Toward an Extreme Fiction." *REL*, IV, iv (1963), 31–46.

13 MORRIS, Wright. "The Function of Style: Ernest Hemingway." See 13.14.

14 MOTOLA, Gabriel. "Hemingway's Code: Literature and Life." *MFS*, X (1964), 319–329.

15 MULLER, Herbert J. See 3.13.

16 O'FAOLAIN, Sean. "Ernest Hemingway, or Men Without Memories." *The Vanishing Hero: Studies of Novelists in the Twenties*. London: Eyre and Spottiswoode, 1956, 137–165. [43-UL]

17 OLDSEY, Bern. "The Snows of Ernest Hemingway." *WSCL*, IV (1963), 172–198.

18 OPPEL, Horst. "Hemingway's *Across the River and into the Trees*." See 56.11.

19 PAOLINI, Pier Francesco. "The Hemingway of the Major Works." See 56.11.

20 PARKER, Stephen Jan. "Hemingway's Revival in the Soviet Union: 1955–1962." *AL*, XXXV (1964), 485–501.

21 PLIMPTON, George. "The Art of Fiction, XXI: Hemingway." *ParisR*, no. 18 (1958), 61–89. Repr. in 13.16 and 56.11. [Interview with Hemingway.]

22 PRAZ, Mario. "Hemingway in Italy." *PR*, XV (1948), 1086–1100. Also in 56.11.

1 RAHV, Philip. "Hemingway in the Early 1950's." *The Myth and the Power-house.* New York: Farrar, Straus & Giroux, 1965, 193–201. [On *Across the River and into the Trees.*] [N-291-Noon]

2 RAHV, Philip. "The Social Muse and the Great Kudu." *PR*, IV (1937), 16–20.

3 ROSENFELD, Isaac. "A Farewell to Hemingway." *KR*, XIII (1951), 147–155. [On *Across the River.*]

4 ROUCH, John S. "Jake Barnes as Narrator." *MFS*, XI (1966), 361–370.

5 RUSSELL, H. K. "The Catharsis in *A Farewell to Arms.*" *MFS*, I (Aug., 1955), 25–30.

6 SANDERS, David. "Ernest Hemingway's Spanish Civil War Experience." *AQ*, XII (1960), 133–143.

7 SAVAGE, D. S. "Ernest Hemingway." *HudR*, I (1948), 380–401. Reprinted in Savage, *The Withered Branch.* London: Eyre and Spottiswoode, 1950, 23–43.

8 SCHORER, Mark. "The Background of a Style." *KR*, III (1941), 101–105. Also in 56.10.

9 SCHWARTZ, Delmore. "Ernest Hemingway's Literary Situation." *SoR*, III (1938), 769–782. Also in 57.6.

10 SCHWARTZ, Delmore. "The Fiction of Ernest Hemingway." *Perspectives USA*, No. 13 (1955), 70–88.

11 SNELL, George D. See 4.12.

12 SPILKA, Mark. "The Death of Love in *The Sun Also Rises.*" See 14.5, 56.10, 56.11, and 57.13.

13 STALLMAN, R. W. "The Sun Also Rises—But No Bells Ring." See 14.6.

14 STEIN, Gertrude. "Ernest Hemingway and the Post-War Decade." *Atlantic*, CLII (Aug., 1933), 197–208. Repr., with revisions, in Stein, *The Auto-biography of Alice B. Toklas.* New York: Harcourt, Brace, 1933, Chapter 7. [V-133-Vin]

15 STEIN, William Bysshe. "Ritual in Hemingway's 'Big Two-Hearted River'." *TSLL*, I (1960), 555–561.

16 STEPHENS, Robert O. "Hemingway's *Across the River and Into the Trees:* A Reprise." *TexSE*, XXXVII (1958), 92–101.

17 TRILLING, Lionel. "Hemingway and His Critics." *PR*, VI (1939), 52–60. Also in 56.11.

18 VAN GELDER, Robert. "Ernest Hemingway Talks of Work and War." See 14.9. [An interview.]

19 WAGENKNECHT, Edward. See 4.14.

20 WALDMEIR, Joseph. "Confiteor Hominem: Ernest Hemingway's Religion of Man." *PMASAL*, XLII (1956), 277–281. Repr. in 56.10 and 57.13.

21 WARREN, Robert Penn. "Hemingway." *KR*, IX (1947), 1–28. Repr. as introd. to Modern Standard Authors Edition of *A Farewell to Arms.* New York: Scribner, 1949. Also in 12.14 and 14.15.

22 WEBSTER, Harvey Curtis. "Ernest Hemingway: The Pursuit of Death." *TQ*, VII (1964), 149–159.

1 WEEKS, Robert P. "Hemingway and the Spectatorial Attitude." *WHR*, XI (1957), 277–281.

2 WEGELIN, Christof. "Hemingway and the Decline of International Fiction." *SR*, LXXIII (1965), 285–298.

3 WEST, Ray B., Jr. "Ernest Hemingway: Death in the Evening." *AR*, IV (1944), 569–580.

4 WEST, Ray B., Jr. "Ernest Hemingway: The Failure of Sensibility." *SR*, LIII (1945), 120–135. Also in 13.9 and 13.15.

5 Wilson, Edmund. "Hemingway: Gauge of Morale." *The Wound and the Bow: Seven Studies in Literature*. Boston: Houghton Mifflin, 1941, 214–222. [136-GB] Also in 57.6.

6 YOUNG, Philip. "Hemingway and Me." *KR*, XXVIII (1966), 15–37.

7 YOUNG, Philip. "On Dismembering Hemingway." *Atlantic*, CCXVIII, ii (1966), 45–49. [Review-article on Hotchner's *Papa Hemingway*.]

8 YOUNG, Philip. "Our Hemingway Man." *KR*, XXVI (1964), 676–707. [Books by and about Hemingway since 1960.]

Hergesheimer, Joseph (1880–1954)

BIBLIOGRAPHY

9 NAPIER, James J. "Joseph Hergesheimer: A Selected Bibliography, 1913–1945." *BB*, XXIV (1963–64), 45–48, 52, 69–70.

BIOGRAPHICAL AND CRITICAL BOOKS

10 CABELL, James Branch. *Joseph Hergesheimer: An Essay in Interpretation*. New York: The Bookfellows, 1921. [A pamphlet.]

11 JONES, Llewellyn. *Joseph Hergesheimer: The Man and His Books*. New York: Knopf, 1920. [A pamphlet.]

12 LANGFORD, Gerald, ed. *Ingenue Among the Lions: The Letters of Emily Clark to Joseph Hergesheimer*. With introd. Austin, Tex.: Univ. of Texas Press, 1965.

13 MARTIN, Ronald E. *The Fiction of Joseph Hergesheimer*. Philadelphia, Pa.: Univ. of Pennsylvania Press, 1965. [Includes bibliography.]

BIOGRAPHICAL AND CRITICAL ESSAYS

14 BALDWIN, Charles C. See 5.3.

15 BEACH, Joseph Warren. See 7.12.

16 BEACH, Joseph Warren. "Point of View: Hergesheimer." See 3.1.

17 BOYNTON, Percy H. See 5.7.

1 BOYNTON, Percy H. "Joseph Hergesheimer." *EJ*, XVI (1927), 335–345. Reprinted in *More Contemporary Americans*. Chicago: Univ. of Chicago Press, 1927, 137–156.

2 CABELL, James Branch. "In Respect to Joseph Hergesheimer." *Bookman*, L (1919), 267–273.

3 CABELL, James Branch. *Some of Us*. New York: McBride, 1930, 91–104.

4 CABELL, James Branch. *Straws and Prayer-Books*. New York: McBride, 1924, 193–221.

5 HAARDT, Sara. "Joseph Hergesheimer's Methods." *Bookman*, LXIX (1929), 398–403.

6 HARTWICK, Harry. See 6.3.

7 HATCHER, Harlan. See 6.5.

8 KAZIN, Alfred. See 2.13.

9 KELLEY, Leon. "America and Mr. Hergesheimer." *SR*, XL (1932), 171–193.

10 MENCKEN, H. L. "Hergesheimer." *Prejudices: Fifth Series*. New York: Knopf, 1926, 42–49.

11 NAPIER, James J. "Letters of Sinclair Lewis to Joseph Hergesheimer, 1915–1922." *AL*, XXXVIII (1966), 236–246.

12 PRIESTLEY, J. B. "Joseph Hergesheimer, an English View." *Bookman*, LXIII (1926), 272–280.

13 QUINN, Arthur Hobson. See 4.11.

14 VAN DOREN, Carl. See 7.5.

15 VAN GELDER, Robert. "The Curious Retirement of Mr. Hergesheimer." See 14.9. [An interview.]

16 VAN VECHTEN, Carl. "How I Remember Joseph Hergesheimer." *YULG*, XXII (1948), 87–92.

17 WAGENKNECHT, Edward. See 4.14.

18 WEST, Geoffrey. "Joseph Hergesheimer: An Appreciation." *VQR*, VIII (1932), 95–108.

Kerouac, Jack (1922–1969)

BIBLIOGRAPHY

19 CHARTERS, Ann. *A Bibliography of Works by Jack Kerouac*. New York: Phoenix Book Shop, 1967.

BIOGRAPHICAL AND CRITICAL ESSAYS

20 ASKEW, Melvin W. "Quests, Cars, and Kerouac." *UKCR*, XXVIII (1962), 231–240.

21 CHAMPNEY, Freeman. "Beat-up or Beatific." *AR*, XIX (1959), 114–121.

22 DUFFEY, Bernard. "The Three Worlds of Jack Kerouac." See 14.10.

23 FROHOCK, W. M. "Jack Kerouac and the Beats." *Strangers to this Ground: Cultural Diversity in Contemporary American Writing*. Dallas, Tex.: Southern Methodist Univ. Press, 1961, 132–147.

1   GOLD, Herbert. "Hip, Cool, Beat—and Frantic." *Nation,* CLXXXV (Nov. 16, 1957), 349–355.

2   KEROUAC, Jack. "Essentials of Spontaneous Prose," and "Belief and Technique for Modern Prose." See 6.20.

3   KEROUAC, Jack. "The Origins of the Beat Generation." See 6.20.

4   PODHORETZ, Norman. "The Know-Nothing Bohemians." *PR,* XXV (1958), 305–318. Also in 6.20 and 14.1. [On *The Subterraneans* and *On the Road.*]

5   STEVENSON, David L. "James Jones and Jack Kerouac: Novelists of Disjunction." See 12.17.

6   TALLMAN, Warren. "Kerouac's Sound." *ER,* IV (1960), 153–169. Also in 6.20.

7   WEBB, Howard W., Jr. "The Singular Worlds of Jack Kerouac." See 13.12.

Lewis, Sinclair (1885–1951)

BIOGRAPHICAL AND CRITICAL BOOKS

8   DOOLEY, D. J. *The Art of Sinclair Lewis.* Lincoln, Nebr.: Univ. of Nebraska Press, 1967.

9   GREBSTEIN, Sheldon N. *Sinclair Lewis.* New York: Twayne, 1962. [T-14-C&UPS]

10 LEWIS, Grace Hegger. *With Love from Gracie: Sinclair Lewis, 1912–1925.* New York: Harcourt, Brace, 1956. [Memoir by Lewis's first wife.]

11 SCHORER, Mark, ed. *Sinclair Lewis: A Collection of Critical Essays.* Englewood Cliffs, N.J.: Prentice-Hall, 1962. [S-TC-6-Spec]

12 SCHORER, Mark. *Sinclair Lewis: An American Life.* New York: McGraw-Hill, 1961. [7929-Delta-Dell]

13 SCHORER, Mark. *Sinclair Lewis.* UMPAW, No. 27. Minneapolis, Minn.: Univ. of Minnesota Press, 1963. [UMP]

14 SHEEAN, Vincent. *Dorothy and Red.* New York: Houghton Mifflin, 1963. [Lewis and Dorothy Thompson.] [T776-Crest]

15 SHERMAN, Stuart Pratt. *The Significance of Sinclair Lewis.* New York: Harcourt, Brace, 1922. [Pamphlet.]

16 SMITH, Harrison, ed. *From Main Street to Stockholm: Letters of Sinclair Lewis, 1915–1930.* New York: Harcourt, Brace, 1952.

17 VAN DOREN, Carl. *Sinclair Lewis: A Biographical Sketch.* New York: Doubleday, 1933.

BIOGRAPHICAL AND CRITICAL ESSAYS

18 AARON, Daniel. "Sinclair Lewis, *Main Street.*" See 14.7.

19 AUSTIN, Allen. "An Interview with Sinclair Lewis." *UKCR,* XXIV (1958), 199–210.

1 BAKER, Joseph E. "Sinclair Lewis, Plato, and the Regional Escape." *EJ*, XXVIII (1939), 460–472.

2 BECK, Warren. "How Good is Sinclair Lewis?" *CE*, IX (1948), 173–180.

3 BECKER, George J. "Sinclair Lewis: Apostle to the Philistines." *ASch*, XXI (1952), 423–432.

4 BOYNTON, Percy H. "Sinclair Lewis." *EJ*, XVI (1927), 251–260. Repr. in Boynton, *More Contemporary Americans*. Chicago: Univ. of Chicago Press, 1927, 179–198.

5 BROWN, Daniel R. "Lewis's Satire—A Negative Emphasis." *Renascence*, XVIII (1966), 63–72.

6 BROWN, Deming. "Sinclair Lewis: The Russian View." *AL*, XXV (1953), 1–12.

7 CABELL, James Branch. *Some of Us: An Essay in Epitaphs*. New York: McBride, 1930, 61–73.

8 CALVERTON, V. F. "Sinclair Lewis, the Last of the Literary Liberals." *ModM*, VIII (1934), 77–86.

9 CANTWELL, Robert. "Sinclair Lewis." *NewR*, LXXXVIII (Oct. 21, 1936), 298–301. Also in 13.2, 14.15, and 65.11.

10 CARPENTER, Frederic I. "Sinclair Lewis and the Fortress of Reality." *CE*, XVI (1955), 416–423.

11 CONTI, Giuseppi Gadda. "Sinclair Lewis." *SA*, IX (1963), 249–286.

12 FLANAGAN, John T. "A Long Way to Gopher Prairie: Sinclair Lewis's Apprenticehsip." *SWR*, XXXII (1947), 403–413.

13 GEISMAR, Maxwell. "Sinclair Lewis: The Cosmic Bourjoyce." See 5.17 and 14.11.

14 GREBSTEIN, Sheldon. "The Education of a Rebel: Sinclair Lewis at Yale." *NEQ*, XXVIII (1955), 372–382.

15 GREBSTEIN, Sheldon. "Sinclair Lewis's Unwritten Novel." *PQ*, XXXVII (1958), 400–409. [Lewis's labor novel and his failure to complete it.]

16 GURKO, Leo and Miriam. "The Two Main Streets of Sinclair Lewis." *CE*, IV (1943), 288–292.

17 HARTWICK, Harry. See 6.3.

18 HATCHER, Harlan. See 6.5.

19 HICKS, Granville. "Sinclair Lewis and the Good Life." *EJ*, XXV (1936), 265–273.

20 HOFFMAN, Frederick J. "Sinclair Lewis's *Babbitt*." See 6.10.

21 HOLLIS, C. Carroll. "Sinclair Lewis: Reviver of Character." See 13.4. [Lewis's characters and the Theophrastian Character.]

22 JONES, Howard Mumford. "Mr. Lewis's America." *VQR*, VII (1931), 427–432.

23 KAZIN, Alfred. "The New Realism: Sherwood Anderson and Sinclair Lewis." See 2.13 and 65.11.

1   LEWIS, Sinclair. "Breaking into Print." *Colophon*, n.s. II (1937), 217–221.

2   LIPPMANN, Walter. "Sinclair Lewis." See 65.11.

3   MANFRED, Frederick F. "Sinclair Lewis: A Portrait." *ASch*, XXIII (1954), 162–184.

4   MICHAUD, Régis. See 6.17.

5   MILLER, Perry. "The Incorruptible Sinclair Lewis." *Atlantic*, CLXXXVII (Apr., 1951), 30–34.

6   MILLGATE, Michael. "Sinclair Lewis and the Obscure Hero." *SA*, VIII (1962), 111–127.

7   MOORE, Geoffrey. "Sinclair Lewis: A Lost Romantic." See 13.1 and 65.11.

8   MUMFORD, LEWIS, "The America of Sinclair Lewis." *CurH*, XXXIII (1931), 529–533. Also in 65.11.

9   NAPIER, James J. "Letters of Sinclair Lewis to Joseph Hergesheimer." *AL*, XXXVIII (1966), 236–246.

10 PARRINGTON, Vernon L. "Sinclair Lewis: Our Own Diogenes." *Main Currents in American Thought*, III: *The Beginnings of Critical Realism in America*. New York: Harcourt, Brace, 1930, 360–369. Also in 65.11. [HO-23-Hbgr]

11 RICHARDSON, Lyon N. "*Arrowsmith:* Genesis, Development, Versions." *AL*, XXVII (1955), 225–244.

12 RICHARDSON, Lyon N. "Revision in Sinclair Lewis's *The Man Who Knew Coolidge*." *AL*, XXV (1953), 326–333.

13 ROSENBERG, Charles E. "Martin Arrowsmith: The Scientist as Hero." *AQ*, XV (1963), 447–458.

14 SCHORER, Mark. "Sinclair Lewis and the Method of Half-Truths." *EIE*, (1955), 117–144. Also in 13.9. [With special emphasis on *Elmer Gantry*.]

15 STOLBERT, Benjamin. "Sinclair Lewis." *AMer*, LIII (1941), 450–460.

16 TANSELLE, G. Thomas. "Sinclair Lewis and Floyd Dell: Two Views of the Midwest." *TCL*, IX (1964), 175–184.

17 VAN DOREN, Carl. "Sinclair Lewis and Sherwood Anderson." *Century*, CX (1925), 362–369.

18 VAN GELDER, Robert. "Sinclair Lewis Talks of Writing—and Acting." See 14.9. [An interview.]

19 WALDEMAN, Milton. "Sinclair Lewis." *LoM*, XIII (1926), 273–281.

20 WARREN, Dale. "Notes on a Genius: Sinclair Lewis at His Best." *Harper's* CCVIII (Jan., 1954), 61–69. [Recollections by an editor-friend.]

21 WEST, Rebecca. *The Strange Necessity*. New York: Doubleday, Doran, 1928, 295–309. [On *Elmer Gantry*.]

22 WHIPPLE, T. K. "Sinclair Lewis." See 14.12 and 65.11.

Mailer, Norman (1923–   )

BIOGRAPHICAL AND CRITICAL ESSAYS

1   BALDWIN, James. "The Black Boy Looks at the White Boy: Norman Mailer." *Esquire*, LV (1961), 102–106.

2   CORONA, Mario. "Norman Mailer." *SA*, XI (1965), 359–407.

3   DIENSTFREY, Harris. "The Fiction of Norman Mailer." See 13.8.

4   GLICKSBERG, Charles I. "Norman Mailer: The Angry Young Novelist in America." *WSCL*, I (1960), 25–34.

5   GOLDSTONE, Herbert. "The Novels of Norman Mailer." *EJ*, XLV (1956), 113–121.

6   HOFFMAN, FREDERICK J. "Norman Mailer and the Revolt of the Ego: Some Observations on Recent American Literature." *WSCL*, I (1960), 5–12.

7   KRIM, Seymour. "A Hungry Mental Lion." *ER*, IV (1960), 178–185.

8   MUDRICK, Marvin. "Mailer and Styron: Guests of the Establishment." *HudR*, XVII (1964), 346–366.

9   NEWMAN, Paul B. "Mailer: The Jew as Existentialist." *NAR*, II, iii (1965), 48–55.

10   PODHORETZ, Norman. "Norman Mailer: The Embattled Vision." *PR*, XXVI (1959), 371–391. Repr. in 14.1 and 14.10.

11   RAHV, Philip. "Crime Without Punishment." *The Myth and the Powerhouse.* New York: Farrar, Straus & Giroux, 1965, 234–243. [On *An American Dream*.]

12   SCHRADER, George Alfred. "Norman Mailer and the Despair of Defiance." *YR*, LII (1962), 267–280.

13   SOLOTAROFF, Robert. "Down Mailer's Way." *ChiR*, XIX, iii (1967), 11–25.

14   STERN, Richard G. "Hip, Hell, and The Navigator: An Interview with Norman Mailer." *WR*, XXIII (1959), 101–109.

15   TANNER, Tony. "On Norman Mailer." *PR*, XXXIV (1967), 465–471. [Review-essay on *Christians and Cannibals*.]

16   TRILLING, Diana. "The Radical Moralism of Norman Mailer." See 12.17.

17   VOLPE, Edmond L. "James Jones—Norman Mailer." See 13.12.

18   WEBER, Brom. "A Fear of Dying: Norman Mailer's *An American Dream*." *HC*, II, iii (1965), 1–6, 8–11. [A review-article.]

Malamud, Bernard (1914–   )

BIOGRAPHICAL AND CRITICAL BOOKS

19   RICHMAN, Sidney. *Bernard Malamud.* New York: Twayne, 1966.

BIOGRAPHICAL AND CRITICAL ESSAYS

1 ALTER, Robert. "Malamud as Jewish Writer." *Commentary*, XLII, iii (1966), 71–76.

2 BAUMBACH, Jonathan. "The Economy of Love: The Novels of Bernard Malamud." *KR*, XXV (1963), 438–457. Also in 5.4.

3 BELLMAN, Samuel Irving. "Women, Children, and Idiots First: The Transformation Psychology of Bernard Malamud." *Crit*, VII, ii (1965), 123–138.

4 BLUEFARB, Sam. "Bernard Malamud: The Scope of Caricature." *EJ*, XXIII (1964), 319–326.

5 GOLDMAN, Mark. "Bernard Malamud's Comic Vision and the Theme of Identity." *Crit*, VII, i (1965), 92–109.

6 HASSAN, Ihab H. See 9.18.

7 HICKS, Granville. "Bernard Malamud." See 12.17.

8 HOYT, Charles A. "Bernard Malamud and the New Romanticism." See 13.12.

9 KLEIN, Marcus. "Bernard Malamud: The Sadness of Goodness." See 6.14.

10 LEER, Norman. "Three American Novels and Contemporary Society: A Search for Commitment." *WSCL*, III (1962), 67–85. [On *The Assistant*.]

11 MANDEL, Ruth B. "Bernard Malamud's *The Assistant* and *A New Life:* Ironic Affirmation." *Crit*, VII, ii (1965), 110–121.

12 MARCUS, Steven. "The Novel Again." *PR*, XXIX (1962), 171–195. [Treats Malamud at length.]

13 MELLARD, James M. "Malamud's Novels: Four Versions of Pastoral." *Crit*, IX, ii (1967), 5–19.

14 RATNER, Marc L. "Style and Humanity in Malamud's Fiction." *MR*, V (1964), 663–683.

15 ROVIT, Earl H. "Bernard Malamud and the Jewish Literary Tradition." *Crit*, III (1960), 3–10.

16 SHEAR, Walter. "Culture Conflict in *The Assistant*." *MQ*, VII (1966), 367–380.

17 SIEGEL, Ben. "Victims in Motion: Bernard Malamud's Sad and Bitter Clowns." *NR*, V (1962), 69–80. Also in 14.10.

18 SOLOTAROFF, Theodore. "Bernard Malamud's Fiction: The Old Life and the New." *Commentary*, XXXIII (1962), 197–204.

19 WASSERMAN, Earl R. "*The Natural:* Malamud's World Ceres." *CRAS*, IX (1965), 438–460.

Marquand, John P. (1893–1960)

BIBLIOGRAPHY

1   WHITE, William. "John P. Marquand: A Preliminary Checklist." *BB*, XIX (1949), 268–271.

2   WHITE, William. "John P. Marquand Since 1950." *BB*, XXI (1956), 230–234. [Bibliography.]

BIOGRAPHICAL AND CRITICAL BOOKS

3   GROSS, John J. *John P. Marquand.* New York: Twayne, 1963. [T-33-C&UPS]

4   HAMBURGER, Philip. *J. P. Marquand, Esquire.* Boston: Houghton Mifflin, 1952. [A series of "Profiles" originally in *NY*.] [137-Chart]

5   HOLMAN, C. Hugh. *John P. Marquand.* UMPAW, No. 46. Minneapolis, Minn.: Univ. of Minnesota Press, 1965. [UMP]

BIOGRAPHICAL AND CRITICAL ESSAYS

6   AUCHINCLOSS, Louis. *Reflections of a Jacobite.* Boston, Mass.: Houghton Mifflin, 1961, 139–155.

7   BEACH, Joseph Warren. "John P. Marquand: The Moonlight of Culture." See 5.5.

8   BOYNTON, Percy Holmes. "The Novel of Puritan Decay: From Mrs. Stowe to John Marquand." *NEQ*, XIII (1940), 626–637. Also in 5.7.

9   BRADY, Charles A. "John Phillips Marquand: Martini-Age Victorian." See 13.4.

10   BRICKELL, Herschel. "Miss Glasgow and Mr. Marquand." *VQR*, XVII (1941), 405–417.

11   BUTTERFIELD, Roger. "John P. Marquand: America's Famous Novelist of Manners." *Life*, XVII (July 31, 1944), 64–73. [Important biographical source.]

12   GOODWIN, George, Jr. "The Last Hurrahs: George Apley and Frank Skeffington." *MR*, I (1960), 461–471.

13   GREENE, George. "A Tunnel from Persepolis: The Legacy of John Marquand." *QQ*, LXXIII (1966), 345–356.

14   GURKO, Leo. "The High-Level Formula of John P. Marquand." *ASch*, XXI (1952), 443–453.

15   HATCHER, Harlan. "John Phillips Marquand." *CE*, I (1939), 107–118; *EJ*, XXVIII (1939), 507–518.

1 HICKS, Granville. "Marquand of Newburyport." *Harpers*, CC (Apr., 1950), 49–72, 101–108.

2 MARQUAND, John P. "Apley, Wickford Point, and Pulham: My Early Struggles." *Atlantic*, CXCVIII (Sept., 1956), 71–76.

3 OPPENHEIMER, Franz M. "Lament for Unbought Grace: The Novels of John P. Marquand." *AR*, XVIII (1958), 41–61.

4 VAN GELDER, Robert. "Marquand Unburdens Himself." See 14.9.

McCarthy, Mary (1912–   )

BIOGRAPHICAL AND CRITICAL BOOKS

5 GRUMBACH, Doris. *The Company She Kept*. New York: Coward-McCann, 1967. [A controversial biography.]

6 MC KENZIE, Barbara. *Mary McCarthy*. New York: Twayne, 1967.

BIOGRAPHICAL AND CRITICAL ESSAYS

7 AUCHINCLOSS, Louis. See 12.16.

8 CHAMBERLAIN, John. "The Novels of Mary McCarthy." See 12.17.

9 KAUFFMAN, Stanley. "Miss McCarthy's Era." *NewR*, CXLIV (Aug. 31, 1963), 25–30. [Essay-review on *The Group*.]

10 MATHEWSON, Ruth. "The Vassar Joke." *CUF*, VI, iv (1963), 10–16. [On *The Group*.]

11 MC CARTHY, Mary. "Characters in Fiction." *PR*, XXVIII (1961), 171–191.

12 MC CARTHY, Mary. "Letter to a Translator: About *The Group*." *Encounter*, XXIII (1964), 69–71, 74–76.

13 NIEBUHR, Elisabeth. "The Art of Fiction, XXVII: Mary McCarthy." *Paris R*, No. 27 (1962), 58–94. Repr. in 13.16. [An interview.]

14 PODHORETZ, Norman. "John O'Hara and Mary McCarthy." See 14.1.

15 SCHLUETER, Paul. "The Dissections of Mary McCarthy." See 13.12.

McCullers, Carson (1917–1967)

BIBLIOGRAPHY

16 PHILLIPS, R. S. "Carson McCullers: 1956–1964: A Selective Checklist." *BB*, XXIV (1964), 113–116.

17 STEWART, Stanley. "Carson McCullers, 1940–1956: A Selected Checklist." *BB*, XXII (1959), 182–185.

BIOGRAPHICAL AND CRITICAL BOOKS

1 EVANS, Oliver. *Carson McCullers: Her Life and Work*. London: Peter Owen, 1965.

BIOGRAPHICAL AND CRITICAL ESSAYS

2 BALDANZA, Frank. "Plato in Dixie." *GaR*, XII (1958), 151–167.

3 DURHAM, Frank. "God and No God in *The Heart is a Lonely Hunter*." *SAQ*, LVI (1956), 494–499.

4 EMERSON, Donald. "The Ambiguities of *Clock Without Hands*." *WSCL*, III (1962), 15–28.

5 EVANS, Oliver. "The Achievement of Carson McCullers." *EJ*, LI (1962), 301–308.

6 EVANS, Oliver. "The Case of Carson McCullers." *GaR*, XVIII (1964), 40–45.

7 EVANS, Oliver. "The Case of the Silent Singer: A Revaluation of *The Heart is a Lonely Hunter*." *GaR*, XIX (1965), 188–203.

8 EVANS, Oliver. "The Theme of Spiritual Isolation in Carson McCullers." *New World Writing*. First Mentor Selection (1952), 297–310. Also in 14.3.

9 FELHEIM, Marvin. "Eudora Welty and Carson McCullers." See 13.12.

10 FOLK, Barbara N. "The Sweet Sad Music of Carson McCullers." *GaR*, XVI (1962), 202–209.

11 HASSAN, Ihab H. "Carson McCullers: The Alchemy of Love and Aesthetics of Pain." *MFS*, V (1959), 311–326. Also in 9.18 and 14.10.

12 KOHLER, Dayton. "Carson McCullers: Variations on A Theme." *EJ*, XL (1951), 415–422; *CE*, XIII (1951), 1–8.

13 LUBBERS, Klaus. "The Necessary Order: A Study of Theme and Structure in Carson McCuller's Fiction." *JA*, VIII (1963), 187–204.

14 MC PHERSON, Hugo. "Carson McCullers: Lonely Huntress." *TamR*, no. 11 (1959), 28–40.

15 MOORE, Jack B. "Carson McCullers: The Heart is a Timeless Hunter." *TCL*, XI (1965), 76–81.

16 PHILLIPS, Robert S. "The Gothic Architecture of *The Member of the Wedding*." *Renascence*, XVI (1964), 59–72.

17 SCHORER, Mark. "McCullers and Capote: Basic Patterns." See 12.17.

18 VICKERY, John B. "Carson McCullers: A Map of Love." *WSCL*, I (1960), 13–24.

Miller, Henry (1891–)

BIBLIOGRAPHY

1 MOORE, Thomas H., ed. *Bibliography of Henry Miller*. Minneapolis, Minn.: Henry Miller Lit. Soc., 1961.

2 RENKEN, Maxine. "Bibliography of Henry Miller: 1945–1961." *TCL*, VII (1962), 180–190.

3 RILEY, Esta Lou. *Henry Miller: An Informal Bibliography, 1924–1960*, Fort Hays, Kansas: Fort Hays Kansas State College, 1962. [Writings by and about Miller.]

BIOGRAPHICAL AND CRITICAL BOOKS

4 BAXTER, Annette K. *Henry Miller, Expatriate. Critical Essays in English and American Literature*, No. 5. Pittsburgh, Pa.: Univ. of Pittsburgh Press, 1961 (Orig.). [Pitts]

5 DURRELL, Lawrence, Alfred PERLÈS, and Henry MILLER. *Art and Outrage: A Correspondence About Henry Miller between Alfred Perlès and Lawrence Durrell*. With an intermission by Henry Miller. New York: Dutton, 1961.

6 FRAENKEL, Michael. *The Genesis of "The Tropic of Cancer."* Berkeley, Calif.: Bern Porter, 1946.

7 GORDON, William A. *The Mind and Art of Henry Miller*. Foreword by Lawrence Durrell. Baton Rouge, La.: Louisiana State Univ. Press, 1967.

8 PERLÈS, Alfred. *My Friend Henry Miller: An Intimate Biography*. New York: John Day, 1956.

9 STUHLMANN, Gunther, ed. *Henry Miller's Letters to Anaïs Nin*. With introd. New York: Putnam, 1965.

10 WICKES, George. *Henry Miller*. UMPAW, No. 56. Minneapolis, Minn.: Univ. of Minnesota Press, 1966. [UMP]

11 WICKES, George, ed. *Henry Miller and the Critics*. Carbondale, Ill.: Southern Illinois Univ. Press, 1963. [Essays by various hands.]

12 WICKES, George, ed. *Lawrence Durrell and Henry Miller: A Private Correspondence*. New York: Dutton, 1963.

13 WIDMER, Kingsley. *Henry Miller*. New York: Twayne, 1963. [T-44-C&UPS]

BIOGRAPHICAL AND CRITICAL ESSAYS

14 DURRELL, Lawrence. "Studies in Genius: VIII—Henry Miller." *Horizon*, XX (1949), 45–61.

1 FOWLIE, Wallace. "Shadow of Doom: An Essay on Henry Miller." *Accent*, V (1944), 49–53.

2 HOFFMAN, Frederick J. See 10.4.

3 KLEINE, Don. "Innocence Forbidden: Henry Miller in the Tropics." *PrS*, XXXIII (1959), 125–130.

4 MAINE, Harold. "Henry Miller: Bigotry's Whipping Boy." *ArQ*, VII (1951), 197–208.

5 MITCHELL, Edward B. "Artists and Artists: The 'Aesthetics' of Henry Miller." *TSLL*, VIII (1966), 103–115.

6 MORAVIA, Alberto. "Two American Writers (1949)." *SR*, LXVIII (1960), 473–481. [On Miller and Capote.]

7 MULLER, Herbert J. "The Worlds of Henry Miller." *KR*, II (1940), 312–318.

8 PERLÈS, Alfred. "Henry Miller in Villa Seurat." *L&LT*, XLI (1944), 148–156.

9 RAHV, Philip. "Henry Miller." *Image and Idea*. Norfolk, Conn.: New Directions, 1949, 144–150.

10 REXROTH, Kenneth. "Reality of Henry Miller." *Bird in the Bush: Obvious Essays*. New York: New Directions, 1959, 154–167. [NDP-80-New]

11 SHAPIRO, Karl. "Greatest Living Author." *In Defense of Ignorance*. New York: Random House, 1960, 313–338. [V275-Vin]

12 TRASCHEN, Isadore. "The Ego and I." *SAQ*, LXV (1966), 345–354.

13 WEST, Herbert Faulkner. "The Strange Case of Henry Miller." *The Mind on the Wing*. New York: Coward-McCann, 1947, 115–138.

14 WICKES, George. "Henry Miller." See 13.16. [A *Paris Review* interview.]

15 WICKES, George. "Henry Miller at Seventy." *ClareQ*, IX (1962), 5–20.

16 WILSON, Edmund. "Twilight of the Expatriates." See 14.14.

Morris, Wright (1910–   )

BIBLIOGRAPHY

17 LINDEN, Stanton J. and David MADDEN. "A Wright Morris Bibliography." *Crit*, IV (1962), 77–87.

BIOGRAPHICAL AND CRITICAL BOOKS

18 MADDEN, David. *Wright Morris*. New York: Twayne, 1964. [T-71-C&UPS]

BIOGRAPHICAL AND CRITICAL ESSAYS

1 BAUMBACH, Jonathan. "Wake Before Bomb: *Ceremony in Lone Tree*." *Crit*, IV, iii (1962), 56–71. Also in 5.4.

2 BLUEFARB, Sam. "Point of View: An Interview with Wright Morris." *Accent*, XIX (1959), 34–46.

3 BOOTH, Wayne C. "The Two Worlds in the Fiction of Wright Morris." *SR*, LXV (1957), 375–399.

4 CARPENTER, Frederic Ives. "Wright Morris and the Territory Ahead." *CE*, XXI (1959), 147–156.

5 GARRETT, George. "Morris the Magician: A Look at *In Orbit*." *HC*, IV, iii (1967), 1–12.

6 HUNT, John W., Jr. "The Journey Back: The Early Novels of Wright Morris." *Crit*, V (1962), 41–60.

7 KLEIN, Marcus. "Wright Morris: The American Territory." See 6.14.

8 MADDEN, David. "The Great Plains in the Novels of Wright Morris." *Crit*, IV, iii (1962), 5–23.

9 MADDEN, David. "The Hero and the Witness in Wright Morris's *Field of Vision*." *PrS*, XXXIV (1960), 263–278.

10 MORRIS, Wright. "Letter to a Young Critic." *MR*, VI (1964–65), 93–100.

11 MORRIS, Wright. "National Book Award Address." *Crit*, IV (1962), 72–75.

12 MORRIS, Wright. "The Origin of a Species, 1942–1957." *MR*, VII (1966), 121–135. [On his own fiction.]

13 TRACHTENBERG, Alan. "The Craft of Vision." *Crit*, IV, iii (1962), 41–55.

14 TUCKER, Martin. "The Landscape of Wright Morris." *LHR*, No. 7 (1954), 43–51.

15 WATERMAN, Arthur E. "The Novels of Wright Morris: An Escape from Nostalgia." *Crit*, IV, iii (1962), 24–40.

Nabokov, Vladimir (1899–   )

BIBLIOGRAPHY

16 BRYER, Jackson R, and Thomas J. BERGIN, Jr. "Vladimir Nabokov's Critical Reputation in English: A Note and a Checklist." *WSCL*, VIII (1967), 312–364.

BIOGRAPHICAL AND CRITICAL BOOKS

17 FIELD, Andrew. *Nabokov: His Life in Art*. Boston, Mass.: Little, Brown, 1967.

1 *Speak Memory: A Memoir Revisited.* New York: Putnam, 1966. [Revised edition of Nabokov's memoir, first published in 1951 under the title *Conclusive Evidence.*]

2 STEGNER, S. Page. *Escape into Aesthetics: The Art of Vladimir Nabokov.* New York: Dial Press, 1967.

BIOGRAPHICAL AND CRITICAL ESSAYS

3 ALDRIDGE, A. Owen. "*Lolita* and *Les Liaisons Dangereuses.*" *WSCL*, II (1961), 20–26.

4 ANDERSON, Quentin. "Nabokov in Time." *NewR*, CLIV (June 4, 1966), 23–28. [On *Pale Fire.*]

5 APPEL, Alfred, Jr. "An Interview with Vladimir Nabokov." *WSCL*, VIII (1967), 127–152.

6 APPEL, Alfred, Jr. "*Lolita:* The Springboard of Parody." *WSCL*, VIII (1967), 204–241.

7 APPEL, Alfred, Jr. "Nabokov's Puppet Show." *NewR*, CLVI (Jan. 14, 1967), 27–30; (Jan. 21, 1967), 25–32. [A review-article occasioned by publication of *Speak, Memory.*]

8 BRICK, Allan. "The Madman in His Cell: Joyce, Beckett, Nabokov and the Stereotypes." *MR*, I (1959), 40–55. [On *Lolita.*]

9 BROWN, Clarence. "Nabokov's Pushkin and Nabokov's Nabokov." *WSCL*, VIII (1967), 280–293. [Relation of Nabokov's Pushkin translation to his fiction.]

10 DEMBO, L. S. "Vladimir Nabokov, An Introduction." *WSCL*, VIII (1967), 111–126.

11 DILLARD, R. H. W. "Not Text, But Texture: The Novels of Vladimir Nabokov." *HC*, III iii (1966), 1–12. [Review-essay, on *Despair.*]

12 DUPEE, F. W. "The Coming of Nabokov." "*The King of Cats*" *and Other Remarks on Writers and Writing.* New York: Farrar, Straus & Giroux, 1965, 117–141. [On *Lolita* and *The Gift.*]

13 FIELD, Andrew. "The Artist as Failure in Nabokov's Early Prose." *WSCL*, VIII (1967), 165–173.

14 GREEN, Martin. "American Rococo: Salinger and Nabokov." *Reappraisals: Some Commonsense Readings in American Literature.* New York: Avon, 1965, 211–229.

15 GREEN, Martin. "The Morality of Lolita." *KR*, XXVIII (1966), 352–377.

16 GROSSHANS, Henry. "Vladimir Nabokov and the Dream of Old Russia." *TSLL*, VII (1966), 401–409.

17 HANDLEY, Jack. "To Die in English." *NR*, VI (1963), 23–40. [On *Pale Fire.*]

18 HAYMAN, John G. "After 'Lolita'—A Conversation with Vladimir Nabokov—with Digressions." *TC*, CLXVI (1959), 444–450.

19 IVASK, George. "The World of Vladimir Nabokov." *RusR*, XX (1961), 134–142.

1 JOHNSON, W. R. *"The Real Life of Sebastian Knight."* *CM*, IV (1963), 111–114.

2 JOSIPOVICI, G. D. *"Lolita:* Parody and the Pursuit of Beauty." *CritQ*, VI (1964), 35–48.

3 KERMODE, Frank. "Aesthetic Bliss." *Encounter*, XIV (June, 1960), 81–86. [Review-essay on *Bend Sinister.*]

4 KOSTELANETZ, Richard. "Nabokov's Obtuse Fool." See 13.8.

5 LEE, L. L. *"Bend Sinister:* Nabokov's Political Dream." *WSCL*, VIII (1967), 193–203.

6 LEE, L. L. "Vladimir Nabokov's Great Spiral of Being." *WHR*, XVIII (1964), 225–236.

7 LYONS, John O. *Pale"* Fire and the Fine Art of Annotation." *WSCL*, VIII (1967), 242–249.

8 MACDONALD, DWIGHT. "Virtuosity Rewarded or Dr. Kinbote's Revenge." *PR*, XXIX (1962), 437–442. [On *Pale Fire.*]

9 MC CARTHY, Mary. "A Bolt from the Blue." *NewR*, CLXVI (June 4, 1962), 21–27. Repr. in *Encounter*, XIX (Oct., 1962), 71–72, 74, 76–78, 80–82, 84. [On *Pale Fire.*]

10 MERIVALE, Patricia. "The Flaunting of Artifice in Vladimir Nabokov and Jorge Luis Borges." *WSCL*, VIII (1967), 294–309.

11 MITCHELL, Charles. "Mythic Seriousness in *Lolita.*" *TSLL*, V (1963), 329–343.

12 NABOKOV, Vladimir. "On a Book Entitled *Lolita.*" *AnRev*, No. 2 (1957) 105–112. Also in *Encounter*, XII (April, 1959), 73–76.

13 NABOKOV, Vladimir. *"Playboy* Interview: Vladimir Nabokov." *Playboy*, XI (Jan., 1964), 35–41, 44–45.

14 Nabokov Special Number. *WSCL*, VIII (1967). [Essays by L. S. Dembo, Gleb Struve, Andrew Field, Claire Rosenfield, L. L. Lee, Alfred Appel, Jr., John O. Lyons, Carol T. Williams, Simon Karlinsky, Clarence Brown, Patricia Merivale, and an interview with Nabokov conducted by Alfred Appel, Jr.; also a "Selected Bibliography of Nabokov's Work" and "Vladimir Nabokov's Critical Reputation in English: A Note and a Checklist," by Jackson R. Bryer and Thomas J. Bergin, Jr.]

15 PRYCE-JONES, Alan. "The Fabulists World: Vladimir Nabokov." See 12.17.

16 ROSENFIELD, Claire. *"Despair* and the Lust for Immortality." *WSCL*, VIII (1967), 174–192.

17 ROUGEMONT, Denis de. *"Lolita,* or Scandal." *Love Declared—Essays on the Myths of Love*. Trans. by Richard Howard. New York: Pantheon, 1963, 48–54.

18 SLONIM, Marc. " 'Doctor Zhivago' and 'Lolita'." *ILA*, No. 2 (1959), 213–225.

19 STERN, Richard G. *"Pnin* and the Dust-Jacket." *PrS*, XXXI (1957), 161–164.

20 STRUVE, Gleb. "Notes on Nabokov as a Russian Writer." *WSCL*, VIII (1967), 153–164.

1 TRILLING, Lionel. "The Last Lover: Vladimir Nabokov's *Lolita*." *Encounter*, XI (1958), 9–19.

2 UPDIKE, John. "Grandmaster Nabokov." *NewR*, CLI (Sept. 26, 1964), 15–18. [On *The Defense*.]

3 WAIN, John. "Nabokov's Beheading." *NewR*, CLXI (Dec. 21, 1959), 17–19. [On *Invitation to a Beheading*.]

4 WILLIAMS, Carol T. "Nabokov's Dialectical Structure." *WSCL*, VIII (1967), 250–267.

5 WILLIAMS, Carol T. " 'Web of Sense': *Pale Fire* in the Nabokov Canon." *Crit*, VI, iii (1963), 29–45.

O'Connor, Flannery (1925–1964)

BIBLIOGRAPHY

6 WEDGE, George F. "Two Bibliographies: Flannery O'Connor, J. F. Powers." *Crit*, II (1958), 59–70.

BIOGRAPHICAL AND CRITICAL BOOKS

7 DRAKE, Robert. *Flannery O'Connor*. CWCP. Grand Rapids, Mich.: Eerdmans, 1966. [Includes bibliography.]

8 FRIEDMAN, Melvin J. and Lewis A. LAWSON, eds. *The Added Dimension: The Art and Mind of Flannery O'Connor*. New York: Fordham Univ. Press, 1966. [Essays by various hands and extensive bibliography.]

9 HYMAN, Stanley Edgar. *Flannery O'Connor*. UMPAW, No. 54. Minneapolis, Minn.: Univ. of Minnesota Press, 1966. [UMP]

BIOGRAPHICAL AND CRITICAL ESSAYS

10 BAUMBACH, Jonathan. "The Creed of God's Grace: The Fiction of Flannery O'Connor." *GaR*, XVII (1963), 334–346. Also in 5.4.

11 COLEMAN, Richard. "Flannery O'Connor: A Scrutiny of Two Forms of her Many-Leveled Art." *Phoenix*, No. 1 (1966), 30–66.

12 DETWEILER, Robert. "The Curse of Christ in Flannery O'Connor's Fiction." *CLS*, II (1966), 235–245.

13 DRAKE, Robert. " 'The Bleeding Stinking Mad Shadow of Jesus' in the Fiction of Flannery O'Connor." *CLS*, III (1966), 183–196.

14 FERRIS, Sumner J. "The Outside and the Inside: Flannery O'Connor's *The Violent Bear It Away*." *Crit*, IV (1961), 11–19.

15 FITZGERALD, Robert. Introduction. Flannery O'Connor, *Everything That Rises Must Converge*. New York: Farrar, Straus, & Giroux, 1965, vii–xxxiv. [Important biographical and critical essay.]

16 FRIEDMAN, Melvin J. "Flannery O'Connor: Another Legend in Southern Fiction." *EJ*, LI (1962), 233–243. Also in 14.10.

1 GORDON, Caroline. "Flannery O'Connor's *Wise Blood*." *Crit*, II (1958), 3–10.

2 HART, Jane. "Strange Earth: The Stories of Flannery O'Connor." *GaR*, XII (1958), 215–222.

3 HAWKES, John. "Flannery O'Connor's Devil." *SR*, LXX (1962), 395–407.

4 LAWSON, Lewis A. "Flannery O'Connor and the Grotesque: *Wise Blood*." *Renascence*, XVIII (1965), 137–147, 156.

5 MC COWN, Robert. "Flannery O'Connor and the Reality of Sin." *CathW*, CLXXXVIII (1959), 285–291.

6 MEADOR, Margaret. "Flannery O'Connor: Literary Witch." *ColQ*, X (1962), 377–386.

7 NOLDE, Sister M. Simon. "*The Violent Bear It Away:* A Study in Imagery." *XUS*, I (1962), 180–194.

8 QUINN, Sister M. Bernetta. "View from a Rock: The Fiction of Flannery O'Connor and J. F. Powers." *Crit*, II (1958), 19–27.

9 RUBIN, Louis D., Jr. "Flannery O'Connor: A Note on Literary Fashions." *Crit*, II (1958), 11–18.

10 SMITH, J. Oates. "Ritual and Violence in Flannery O'Connor." *Thought*, XLI (1966), 545–560.

11 STELZMANN, RAINULF. "Shock and Orthodoxy: An Interpretation of Flannery O'Connor's Novels and Short Stories." *XUS*, II (1963), 4–21.

12 STERN, Richard. "Flannery O'Connor: A Remembrance and Some Letters." *Shenandoah*, XVI, ii (1965), 5–10.

O'Hara, John (1905–)

BIOGRAPHICAL AND CRITICAL BOOKS

13 CARSON, Edward R. *The Fiction of John O'Hara*. *CEEAL*, No. 7. Pittsburgh, Pa.: Univ. of Pittsburgh Press, 1961 (Orig.). [Pitts]

14 GREBSTEIN, Sheldon Norman. *John O'Hara*. New York: Twayne, 1966.

BIOGRAPHICAL AND CRITICAL ESSAYS

15 AUCHINCLOSS, Louis. *Reflections of a Jacobite*. Boston: Houghton Mifflin, 1961, 139–155.

16 BIER, Jesse. "O'Hara's *Appointment in Samarra:* His First and Only Real Novel." *CE*, XXV (1963), 135–141.

17 PODHORETZ, Norman. "John O'Hara and Mary McCarthy." See 14.1.

18 VAN GELDER, Robert. "John O'Hara, Who Talks Like His Stories." See 14.9. [An interview.]

Porter, Katherine Anne (1890–)

BIBLIOGRAPHY

1 SCHWARTZ, Edward. "Katherine Anne Porter: A Critical Bibliography." *BNYPL*, LVII (1953), 211–247. [Includes an introduction by Robert Penn Warren.]

2 SYLVESTER, William A. "Selected and Critical Bibliography of the Uncollected Works of Katherine Anne Porter." *BB*, XIX (1947), 36.

BIOGRAPHICAL AND CRITICAL BOOKS

3 HENDRICK, George. *Katherine Anne Porter*. New York: Twayne, 1965. [T-90-C&UPS]

4 MOONEY, Harry J., Jr. *The Fiction and Criticism of Katherine Anne Porter*. Rev. ed. *CEEAL*, No. 2. Pittsburgh, Pa.: Univ. of Pittsburgh Press, 1962. [Pitts]

5 NANCE, William L., S.M. *Katherine Anne Porter and the Art of Rejection*. Chapel Hill, N.C.: Univ. of North Carolina Press, 1964.

6 WEST, Ray B., Jr. *Katherine Anne Porter*. UMPAW, No. 28. Minneapolis, Minn.: Univ. of Minnesota Press, 1963. [UMP]

BIOGRAPHICAL AND CRITICAL ESSAYS

7 ALEXANDER, Jean. "Katherine Anne Porter's Ship in the Jungle." *TCL*, XI (1966), 179–188. [On *Ship of Fools*.]

8 ALLEN, Charles G. "Katherine Anne Porter: Psychology as Art." *SWR*, XLI (1956), 223–230.

9 CURLEY, Daniel. "Katherine Anne Porter: The Larger Plan." *KR*, XXV (1963), 671–695.

10 HARTLEY, Lodwick. "Dark Voyagers: A Study of Katherine Anne Porter's *Ship of Fools*." *UR*, XXX (1963), 83–94.

11 HARTLEY, Lodwick. "Katherine Anne Porter." *SR*, XLVIII (1940), 201–216.

12 HEILMAN, Robert B. "*Ship of Fools:* Notes on Style." *FQ*, (LaSalle Coll.), XII (1962), 46–55.

13 HERTZ, Robert Neil. "Sebastian Brant and Porter's *Ship of Fools*." *MQ*, VI (1965), 389–401.

14 JOHNSON, J. W. "Another Look at Katherine Anne Porter." *VQR*, XXXVI (1960), 598–613.

15 JOSELYN, Sister M. "On the Making of *Ship of Fools*." *SDR*, I, ii (1964), 46–52.

16 KAPLAN, Charles. "True Witness: Katherine Anne Porter." *ColQ*, VII (1959), 319–327.

1 LIBERMAN, M. M. "The Responsibility of the Novelist: The Critical Reception of *Ship of Fools*." *Criticism*, VIII (1966), 377–388.

2 MILLER, Paul W. "Katherine Anne Porter's *Ship of Fools:* A Masterpiece Manqué." *UR*, XXXII (1965), 151–157.

3 PIERCE, Marvin. "Point of View: Katherine Anne Porter's *Noon Wine*." *OUR*, III (1961), 95–113.

4 PORTER, Katherine Anne. "'Noon Wine': The Sources." *YR*, XLVI (1956), 22–39.

5 RUOFF, James and Del SMITH. "Katherine Anne Porter on *Ship of Fools*." *CE*, XXIV (1963), 396–397. [An interview with Miss Porter.]

6 SCHWARTZ, Edward. "The Way of Dissent: Katherine Anne Porter's Critical Position." *WHR*, VIII (1954), 119–130.

7 SOLOTAROFF, Theodore. "*Ship of Fools* and the Critics." *Commentary*, XXXIV (1962), 277–286.

8 SUTHERLAND, Donald. "Ole Woman River: A Correspondence with Katherine Anne Porter." *SR*, LXXIV (1966), 754–767.

9 THOMPSON, Barbara. "Katherine Anne Porter." See 13.16. [A *Paris Review* interview.]

10 VAN GELDER, Robert. "Katherine Anne Porter at Work." See 14.9.

11 WARREN, Robert Penn. "Katherine Anne Porter (Irony with a Center)." *KR*, IV (1942), 29–42.

12 WESCOTT, Glenway. "Katherine Anne Porter: The Making of a Novel." *Atlantic*, CCIX (Apr., 1962), 43–49.

13 WEST, Ray B., Jr. "Katherine Anne Porter and 'Historic Memory'." *HoR*, VI (1952), 16–27.

14 WEST, Ray B., Jr. "Katherine Anne Porter: Symbol and Theme in 'Flowering Judas'." *Accent*, VII (1947), 182–187.

15 YOUNG, Vernon A. "The Art of Katherine Anne Porter." *NMQR*, XV (1945), 326–341.

Roberts, Elizabeth Madox (1886–1941)

BIOGRAPHICAL AND CRITICAL BOOKS

16 ADAMS, J. Donald, and others. *Elizabeth Madox Roberts: An Appraisal.* New York: Viking, 1938. [A collection of articles and reviews.]

17 CAMPBELL, Harry Modean and Ruel E. FOSTER. *Elizabeth Madox Roberts: American Novelist.* Norman, Okla.: Univ. of Oklahoma Press, 1956.

18 MC DOWELL, Frederick P. W. *Elizabeth Madox Roberts.* New York: Twayne, 1963. [T-38-C&UPS]

19 ROVIT, Earl H. *Herald to Chaos: The Novels of Elizabeth Madox Roberts.* Lexington, Ky.: Univ. of Kentucky Press, 1960.

BIOGRAPHICAL AND CRITICAL ESSAYS

1 ADAMS, J. Donald. "Elizabeth Madox Roberts." *VQR*, XII (1936), 80–90.

2 BUCHAN, Alexander M. "Elizabeth Madox Roberts." *SWR*, XXV (1940), 463–481.

3 CAMPBELL, Harry Modean. "The Poetic Prose of Elizabeth Madox Roberts." *SWR*, XXXIX (1954), 285–297. Also in 81.17.

4 CAMPBELL, Harry Modean. "A Revaluation of Elizabeth Madox Roberts' *The Time of Man* and *The Great Meadow*." *Shenandoah*, V (1954), 42–59. Also in 81.17.

5 DAVIDSON, Donald. "Analysis of Elizabeth Madox Roberts' *A Buried Treasure*." *CrR*, VI (Dec., 1931), 1235–1249.

6 JANNEY, F. Lamar. "Elizabeth Madox Roberts." *SR*, XLV (1937), 388–410.

7 ROVIT, Earl H. "The Great Meadow: Genesis and Exodus." *MissQ*, XI (1958), 1–18.

8 ROVIT, Earl H. "*He Sent Forth A Raven:* The Curse and the Covenant." *MissQ*, XII (1959), 23–45.

9 ROVIT, Earl H. "Recurrent Symbols in the Novels of Elizabeth Madox Roberts." *BUSE*, II (1956), 36–54.

10 VAN DOREN, Mark. "Elizabeth Madox Roberts." *EJ*, XXI (1932), 521–528.

11 WAGENKNECHT, Edward. See 4.14.

12 WARREN, Robert Penn. "Elizabeth Madox Roberts: Life is From Within." *SatR*, XLVI (9 March, 1963), 20–21, 38.

13 WESCOTT, Glenway. "Elizabeth Madox Roberts: A Personal Note." *Bookman*, LXXI (1930), 12–15.

Roth, Philip (1933–)

BIOGRAPHICAL AND CRITICAL ESSAYS

14 DEER, Irving and Harriet. "Philip Roth and the Crisis in American Fiction." *Minnesota Review*, VI (1966), 353–360.

15 ISAAC, Dan. "In Defense of Philip Roth." *ChiR*, XVII, ii–iii (1964), 84–96.

16 LANDIS, Joseph C. "The Sadness of Philip Roth: An Interim Report." *MR*, III (1962), 259–268.

17 ROTH, Philip. "Writing About Jews." *Commentary*, XXXVI (1963), 445–452.

18 ROTH, Philip. "Writing American Fiction." *Commentary*, XXXI (1961), 223–233. [Discusses Bellow, Salinger, Malamud, Gold, among others.]

19 SOLOTAROFF, Theodore. "Philip Roth and the Jewish Moralists." *ChiR*, XIII (1959), 87–99.

Salinger, J. D. (1919–   )

BIBLIOGRAPHY

1   BEEBE, Maurice and Jennifer SPERRY. "Criticism of J. D. Salinger: A Selected Checklist." *MFS*, XII (1966), 377–380.

2   DAVIS, Tom. "J. D. Salinger: A Checklist." *PBSA*, LIII (1959), 69–71.

3   FIENE, Donald M. "J. D. Salinger: A Bibliography." *WSCL*, IV, i (1963), 109–149.

BIOGRAPHICAL AND CRITICAL BOOKS

4   BELCHER, William F. and James W. LEE, eds. *J. D. Salinger and the Critics*. Belmont, Calif.: Wadsworth, 1962. [Controlled research volume.] [Wdwth]

5   FRENCH, Warren. *J. D. Salinger*. New York: Twayne, 1963 [T-40-C& UPS]

6   GRUNWALD, Henry A., ed. *Salinger: A Critical and Personal Portrait*. New York: Harper, 1962. [Essays by various hands.] [CN/13-CN; GC169-PB]

7   GWYNN, Frederick L. and Joseph L. BLOTNER. *The Fiction of J. D. Salinger*. *CEEAL, No. 4*. Pittsburgh, Pa.: Univ. of Pittsburgh Press, 1958. [Pitts]

8   LASER, Marvin and Norman FRUMAN, eds. *Studies in J. D. Salinger*. New York: Odyssey, 1963 (Orig.). [Reviews, essays, and critiques by various hands.] [Odys]

9   MARSDEN, Malcolm M., ed. *If You Really Want to Know: A Catcher Casebook*. Chicago: Scott, Foresman, 1963 (Orig.). [5206-Scott]

10   MILLER, James E., Jr. *J. D. Salinger*. UMPAW, No. 51. Minneapolis, Minn.: Univ. of Minnesota Press, 1965. [UMP]

11   SIMONSON, Harold P. and E. P. HAGER, eds. *Salinger's "Catcher in the Rye": Clamor vs. Criticism*. New York: Heath, 1963 (Orig.). [Heath]

BIOGRAPHICAL AND CRITICAL ESSAYS

12   BARR, Donald. "Ah, Buddy: Salinger." See 12.17.

13   BASKETT, Sam S. "The Splendid/Squalid World of J. D. Salinger." *WSCL*, IV, i (1963), 48–61.

14   BAUMBACH, Jonathan. "The Saint as a Young Man: A Reappraisal of *The Catcher in the Rye*." *MLQ*, XXV (1964), 461–472. Also in 5.4.

15   BLOTNER, Joseph L. "Salinger Now: An Appraisal." *WSCL*, IV, i (1963), 100–108.

1 BRANCH, Edgar M. "Mark Twain and J. D. Salinger: A Study in Literary Continuity." *AQ*, IX (1957), 144–158. Also in 83.6 and 83.8.

2 COSTELLO, Donald P. "The Language of *The Catcher in the Rye*." *AS*, XXXIV (1959), 172–181. Also in 83.8.

3 DAVIS, Tom. "J. D. Salinger: The Sound of One Hand Clapping." *WSCL*, IV (1963), 41–47.

4 DEER, Irving and John H. RANDALL, III. "J. D. Salinger and the Reality Beyond Words." *LHR*, No. 6 (1964), 14–29.

5 FIEDLER, Leslie. "The Eye of Innocence." *No! in Thunder*. Boston: Beacon Press, 1960, 251–291.

6 FIEDLER, Leslie. See 4.9.

7 FRENCH, Warren. "The Phony World and the Nice World." *WSCL*, IV (1963), 21–30.

8 GEISMAR, Maxwell. "The Wise Child and the *New Yorker* School of Fiction." See 13.5 and 83.6.

9 GILES, Barbara. "The Lonely War of J. D. Salinger." *Mainstream*, XII (1959), 2–13.

10 GREEN, Martin. "American Rococo: Salinger and Nabokov." See 13.6.

11 GRUNWALD, Henry A. "The Invisible Man: A Biographical College." See 83.6. [Biographical sketch of Salinger.]

12 GUTWILLIG, Robert. "Everybody's Caught *The Catcher in the Rye*." See 83.8. [The reception of the novel.]

13 HASSAN, Ihab H. "Almost the Voice of Silence: The Later Novelettes of J. D. Salinger." *WSCL*, IV, i (1963), 5–20.

14 HASSAN, Ihab H. "J. D. Salinger: Rare Quixotic Gesture." *WR*, XXI (1957), 261–280. Also in 9.18, 83.6, and 83.8.

15 HAVEMANN, Ernest. "Search for the Mysterious J. D. Salinger." *Life*, LI (Nov. 3, 1961), 129–130, 132–144.

16 HEISERMAN, Arthur and James E. MILLER, Jr. "J. D. Salinger: Some Crazy Cliff." *WHR*, X (1956), 129–137. Also in 83.6 and 83.8.

17 KAPLAN, Charles. "Holden and Huck: The Odysseys of Youth." *CE*, XVIII (1956), 76–80. Also in 83.8.

18 KAZIN, Alfred. "J. D. Salinger: 'Everybody's Favorite!'" *Atlantic*, CCVIII (Aug., 1961), 27–31. Also in 83.6 and 83.8.

19 KINNEY, Arthur F. "J. D. Salinger and the Search for Love." *TSLL*, V (1963), 111–126.

20 LASER, Marvin and Norman FRUMAN. "Salinger: The Early Reviews." See 83.8.

21 LEITCH, David. "The Salinger Myth." See 83.6.

22 LEVINE, Paul. "J. D. Salinger: The Development of the Misfit Hero." *TCL*, IV (1958), 92–99.

1 MALIN, Irving. See 11.3.

2 MARCUS, Fred H. " *'The Catcher in the Rye'*: A Live Circuit." *EJ*, LII (1963), 1–8.

3 MC CARTHY, Mary. "J. D. Salinger's Closed Circuit." *Harpers*, CCXXV (Oct., 1962), 46–48. Also in 83.8. [On *Franny and Zooey*.]

4 MIZENER, Arthur. "The American Hero as Poet: Seymour Glass." See 13.11.

5 MIZENER, Arthur. "The Love Song of J. D. Salinger." *Harpers*, CCXVIII (Feb., 1959), 83–90. Also in 83.6 and 83.8.

6 *Modern Fiction Studies*. J. D. Salinger Special Number. XII (1966). [Essays by various hands and a checklist of Salinger criticism.]

7 O'HARA, J. D. "No Catcher in the Rye." *MFS*, IX (1963), 370–376. Also in 14.11.

8 OLDSEY, Bernard. "The Movies in the Rye." *CE*, XXIII (1961), 209–215.

9 REES, Richard. "The Salinger Situation." See 13.12.

10 RUSSELL, John. "Salinger, From Daumier to Smith." *WSCL*, IV (1963), 70–87.

11 SCHWARTZ, Arthur. "For Seymour—with Love and Judgment." *WSCL*, IV (1963), 88–99.

12 SENG, Peter J. "The Fallen Idol: The Immature World of Holden Caulfield." *CE*, XXIII (1961), 203–209.

13 SLABEY, Robert M. "*The Catcher in the Rye:* Christian Theme and Symbol." *CLAJ*, VI (1963), 170–183.

14 STEINER, George. "The Salinger Industry." *Nation*, CLXXXIX (Nov. 14, 1959), 360–363.

15 STRAUCH, Carl F. "Kings in the Back Row: Meaning Through Structure —A Reading of Salinger's *The Catcher in the Rye*." *WSCL*, II (1961), 5–30. Also in 83.8.

16 STRAUCH, Carl F. "Salinger: The Romantic Background." *WSCL*, IV (1963), 31–40.

17 TROWBRIDGE, Clinton W. "The Symbolic Structure of *The Catcher in the Rye*." *SR*, LXXIV (1966), 681–693.

18 VANDERBILT, Kermit. "Symbolic Resolution in *The Catcher in the Rye:* The Cap, The Carrousel and the American West." *WHR*, XVII (1963), 271–277.

19 WAKEFIELD, Dan. "Salinger and the Search for Love." *New World Writing* (14th Mentor Selection). New York: New American Library, 1958, 68–85. Also in 83.6.

20 WAY, Brian. "A Tight Three-Movement Structure." See 83.8. [Close analysis of the form and structure of *Catcher*.]

21 WIEGAND, William. "J. D. Salinger's Seventy-eight Bananas." *ChiR*, XI, No. 4 (1958), 3–19. Also in 14.10 and 83.6. [The coherence of Salinger's vision.]

22 WIEGAND, William. "The Knighthood of J. D. Salinger." *NewR*, CXLI (Oct. 19, 1959), 19–22. Also in 83.6 and 83.8.

Stein, Gertrude (1874–1946)

BIBLIOGRAPHY

1 HAAS, Robert B. and Donald C. GALLUP. *A Catalogue of the Published and Unpublished Writings of Gertrude Stein.* New Haven, Conn.: Yale Univ. Library, 1941.

2 SAWYER, Julian. *Gertrude Stein: A Bibliography.* New York: Arrow Editions, 1940.

BIOGRAPHICAL AND CRITICAL BOOKS

3 BRINNIN, John Malcolm. *The Third Rose: Gertrude Stein and Her World* Boston: Atlantic, Little, Brown, 1959.

4 HOFFMAN, Frederick J. *Gertrude Stein.* UMPAW No. 10. Minneapolis, Minn.: Univ. of Minnesota Press, 1961. [UMP]

5 HOFFMANN, Michael J. *The Development of Abstractionism in the Writings of Gertrude Stein.* Philadelphia, Pa.: Univ. of Pennsylvania Press, 1965. [Stein's first decade of writing; includes *The Making of Americans.*]

6 MILLER, Rosamond S. *Gertrude Stein: Form and Intelligibility.* New York: Exposition Press, 1949.

7 REID, B. L. *Art by Subtraction: A Dissenting Opinion of Gertrude Stein.* Norman, Okla.: Univ. of Oklahoma Press, 1958.

8 ROGERS, W. G. *When This You See Remember Me.* New York: Rinehart, 1948. [A memoir by an old friend.]

9 SPRIGGE, Elizabeth. *Gertrude Stein: Her Life and Work.* New York: Harper, 1957.

10 STEIN, Leo. *Journey into the Self: Being the Letters, Papers, and Journals of Leo Stein.* Ed. by Edmund Fuller. New York: Crown, 1950. [Gertrude Stein's brother and the companion of her early years abroad.]

11 STEWART, Allegra. *Gertrude Stein and the Present.* Cambridge, Mass.: Harvard Univ. Press, 1967.

12 SUTHERLAND, Donald. *Gertrude Stein: A Biography of Her Works.* New Haven, Conn.: Yale Univ. Press, 1951.

13 SUTHERLAND, Donald. *Two: Gertrude Stein and Her Brother.* New Haven, Conn.: Yale Univ. Press, 1951.

14 TOKLAS, Alice B. *What is Remembered.* New York: Holt, Rinehart & Winston, 1963.

BIOGRAPHICAL AND CRITICAL ESSAYS

15 BRIDGMAN, Richard. " 'Melanctha'." *AL,* XXXIII (1961), 350–359.

16 BURGUM, Edwin Berry. "The Genius of Miss Gertrude Stein." See 8.4.

1 GALLUP, Donald G. "The Making of *The Making of Americans.*" *NewC*, III (1950), 54–74.

2 HOFFMAN, Frederick J "Gertrude Stein: The Method and the Subject " See 4.10.

3 WILSON, Edmund. "Gertrude Stein." *Axel's Castle: A Study in the Imaginative Literature of 1870–1930.* New York: Scribner, 1947, 237–256. [SL12-Scrib]

Steinbeck, John (1902–1969)

BIBLIOGRAPHY

4 BEEBE, Maurice and Jackson R. BRYER. "Criticism of John Steinbeck: A Selected Checklist." *MFS*, XI (1965), 90–103.

5 HAYASHI, Tetsumaro. *John Steinbeck: A Concise Bibliography (1930–1965).* Introd. by Warren French. Metuchen, N.J.: Scarecrow Press, 1967.

6 POWELL, Lawrence Clark. "Toward a Bibliography of John Steinbeck." *Colophon*, new series III (1938), 558–568.

7 STEELE, Joan. "John Steinbeck: A Checklist of Biographical, Critical, and Bibliographical Material." *BB*, XXIV (1965), 149–152, 162–163.

BIOGRAPHICAL AND CRITICAL BOOKS

8 FONTENROSE, Joseph. *John Steinbeck: An Introduction and Interpretation.* New York: Barnes & Noble, 1963.

9 FRENCH, Warren. *John Steinbeck.* New York: Twayne, 1961. [T-2-C&UPS]

10 LISCA, Peter. *The Wide World of John Steinbeck.* New Brunswick, N.J.: Rutgers Univ. Press, 1958.

11 MOORE, Harry Thornton. *The Novels of John Steinbeck: A First Critical Study.* Chicago, Ill.: Normandie House, 1939.

12 TEDLOCK, Ernest W., Jr. and C. V. WICKER, eds. *Steinbeck and His Critics: A Record of Twenty-five Years.* Albuquerque, N.M.: Univ. of New Mexico Press, 1957.

13 WATT, F. W. *John Steinbeck.* New York: Grove Press, 1962.

BIOGRAPHICAL AND CRITICAL ESSAYS

14 BAKER, Howard. "In Praise of the Novel: The Fiction of Huxley, Steinbeck, and Others." *SoR*, V (1940), 778–800.

15 BEACH, Joseph Warren. "John Steinbeck: Journeyman Artist," and "John Steinbeck: Art and Propaganda." See 5.5 and 87.12.

16 BOWRON, Bernard. "*The Grapes of Wrath:* A 'Waggons West' Romance." *ColQ*, III (1954), 84–91. [The relation of Steinbeck's novel to the "Covered Wagon" romance formula.]

17 BOYNTON, Percy H. "John Steinbeck." See 5.7.

1   BRACHER, Frederick. "Steinbeck and the Biological View of Man." *PS*, II (1948), 14–29. Also in 87.12.

2   BURGUM, Edwin Berry. "The Sensibility of John Steinbeck." *S&S*, X (1946), 132–147. Repr. in 8.4 and 87.12.

3   CARLSON, Eric W. "Symbolism in *The Grapes of Wrath.*" *CE*, XIX (1958), 172–175.

4   CALVERTON, V. F. "Steinbeck, Hemingway, and Faulkner." *ModQ*, XI (Feb., 1939), 36–44.

5   CARPENTER, Frederick Ives. "The Philosophical Joads." *CE*, II (1941), 315–325. Also in 87.12.

6   CARPENTER, Frederick Ives. "John Steinbeck: American Dreamer." *SWR*, XXVI (1941), 454–467. Also in 87.12.

7   CHAMPNEY, Freeman. "John Steinbeck, Californian." *AR*, VII (1947), 345–362. Also in 87.12.

8   CORIN, Fernand. "Steinbeck and Hemingway—A Study in Literary Economy." *RLV*, XXIV (1958), 60–75, 153–163.

9   EISINGER, Chester E. "Jeffersonian Agrarianism in *The Grapes of Wrath.*" *UKCR*, XIV (1947), 149–154.

10   FAIRLEY, Barker. "John Steinbeck and the Coming Literature." *SR*, L (1942), 145–161.

11   FRENCH, Warren. "Another Look at *The Grapes of Wrath.*" *ColQ*, III (1955), 337–343. [An answer to Bernard Bowron's essay.]

12   FROHOCK, W. M. "John Steinbeck's Men of Wrath." *SWR*, XXXI (1946), 144–152.

13   GANNETT, Lewis. "John Steinbeck's Way of Writing." Introd. to *The Portable Steinbeck*. Ed. Lewis Gannett. New York: Viking, 1946. Also in 87.12.

14   GEISMAR, Maxwell. "John Steinbeck: Of Wrath or Joy." See 6.1.

15   GIBBS, Lincoln R. "John Steinbeck, Moralist." *AR*, II (1942), 172–184. Also in 87.12.

16   GRIFFIN, Robert J. and William A. FREEDMAN. "Machines and Animals: Pervasive Motifs in *The Grapes of Wrath.*" *JEGP*, LXII (1963) 569–580.

17   HYMAN, Stanley Edgar. "Some Notes on John Steinbeck." *AR*, II (1942), 185–200. Also in 87.12.

18   JONES, Claude E. "Proletarian Writing and John Steinbeck." *SR*, XLVIII (1940), 445–456.

19   KENNEDY, John S. "John Steinbeck: Life Affirmed and Dissolved." See 13.4 and 87.12.

20   LEWIS, R. W. B. "John Steinbeck: The Fitful Daemon." See 13.1 and 13.9.

21   LISCA, Peter. "*The Grapes of Wrath* as Fiction." *PMLA*, LXXII (1957), 296–309. Also in 14.11.

22   LISCA, Peter. "John Steinbeck: A Literary Biography." See 87.12.

1 LISCA, Peter. "Motif and Pattern in *Of Mice and Men.*" *MFS*, II (1956), 228–234.

2 MAGNY, Claude-Edmonde. "*East of Eden.*" *Perspectives USA*, V (1953), 146–152.

3 MAGNY, Claude-Edmonde. "Steinbeck, or the Limits of the Impersonal Novel." See 87.12.

4 METZGER, Charles R. "Steinbeck's Version of the Pastoral." *MFS*, VI (1960), 115–124. [On *Sweet Thursday.*]

5 *Modern Fiction Studies*, XI, i (Spring, 1965). John Steinbeck Number. [Essays by various hands.]

6 MORRIS, Harry. "*The Pearl:* Realism and Allegory." *EJ*, LII (1963), 487–495, 505.

7 NEVIUS, Blake. "Steinbeck: One Aspect." *PS*, III (1949), 302–311. Also in 87.12.

8 POLLOCK, Theodore. "On the Ending of *The Grapes of Wrath.*" *MFS*, IV (1958), 177–178.

9 RASCOE, Burton. "John Steinbeck." *EJ*, XXVII (1938), 205–216. Also in 87.12.

10 RICKETTS, Toni Jackson [Antonia Seixas]. "John Steinbeck and the Non-Teleological Bus." See 87.12. [By Steinbeck's former secretary.]

11 ROSS, Woodburn O. "John Steinbeck: Earth and Stars." See 87.12.

12 ROSS, Woodburn O. "John Steinbeck: Naturalism's Priest." *CE*, X (1949), 432–437. Also in 87.12.

13 SHOCKLEY, Martin. "Christian Symbolism in *The Grapes of Wrath.*" *CE*, XVIII (1956), 87–90. Also in 87.12.

14 SHOCKLEY, Martin. "The Reception of *The Grapes of Wrath* in Oklahoma." *AL*, XV (1944), 351–361. Also in 87.12.

15 SLOCHOWER, Harry. "The Promise of America: John Steinbeck." *No Voice is Wholly Lost.* New York: Creative Age, 1945.

16 SMITH, Thelma M. and Ward L. MINER. "Steinbeck." See 12.3.

17 SNELL, George D. "John Steinbeck." See 4.12.

18 STEINBECK, John. "Critics, Critics, Burning Bright." *SatR*, XXXIII (Nov. 11, 1950), 20–22. Also in 87.12. [On "the writing, production, and reception of the play-novelette *Burning Bright.*"]

19 STEINBECK, John. "Dubious Battle in California." *Nation*, CXLIII (Sept. 12, 1936), 302–304.

20 STEINBECK, John. "My Short Novels." *EJ*, XLIII (1954), 147. Repr. in 87.12.

21 TAYLOR, Walter Fuller. "*The Grapes of Wrath* Reconsidered." *MissQ*, XII (1959), 136–144.

22 WALCUTT, Charles Child. See 12.9.

23 WEEKS, Donald. "Steinbeck Against Steinbeck." *PS*, I (1947), 447–457.

1   WHIPPLE, T. K. "Steinbeck through a Glass, though Brightly." *NewR*, XCVI (Oct. 12, 1938), 274–275. Also in 14.13.

2   WOODRESS, James. "John Steinbeck: Hostage to Fortune." *SAQ*, LXIII (1964), 385–398.

Styron, William (1925–   )

BIBLIOGRAPHY

3   SCHNEIDER, Harold W. "Two Bibliographies: Saul Bellow, William Styron." *Crit*, III (1960), 71–91.

BIOGRAPHICAL AND CRITICAL ESSAYS

4   ALDRIDGE, John W. "The Society of Three Novels." See 12.15. [Includes discussion of *Lie Down in Darkness*.]

5   BAUMBACH, Jonathan. "Paradise Lost: The Novels of William Styron." *SAQ*, LXIII (1964), 207–217. Also in 5.4.

6   BENSON, Alice R. "Techniques in the Twentieth-Century Novel for Relating the Particular to the Universal: *Set This House on Fire*." *PMASAL*, XLVII (1962), 387–394.

7   BRYANT, Jerry H. "The Hopeful Stoicism of William Styron." *SAQ*, LXII (1963), 539–550.

8   DAVIS, Robert Gorham. "The American Individualist Tradition: Bellow and Styron." See 12.17.

9   DAVIS, Robert Gorham. "Styron and the Students." *Crit*, III, iii (1960), 37–46.

10   DEMPSEY, David. "Talk with William Styron." *NYTBR*, (Sept. 9, 1951), 27.

11   FENTON, Charles A. "William Styron and the Age of the Slob." *SAQ*, LIX (1960), 469–476.

12   FOSTER, Richard. "An Orgy of Commerce: William Styron's *Set This House on Fire*." *Crit*, III (1960), 59–70.

13   FRIEDMAN, Melvin J. "William Styron: An Interim Appraisal." *EJ*, L (1961), 149–158, 192.

14   GALLOWAY, David D. "The Absurd Man as a Tragic Hero: The Novels of William Styron." *TSLL*, VI (1965), 512–534. Also in 9.5.

15   GEISMAR, Maxwell. "William Styron: The End of Innocence." See 13.5.

16   HASSAN, Ihab H. "Encounter with Necessity." See 9.18 and 13.8.

17   HAYS, Peter L. "The Nature of Rebellion in *The Long March*." *Crit*, VIII, ii (1966), 70–74.

18   LAWSON, John H. "Styron: Darkness and Fire in the Modern Novel." *Mainstream*, XIII (Oct., 1960), 9–18.

1 LAWSON, Lewis. "Cass Kinsolving: Kierkegaardian Man of Despair." *WSCL*, III (1962), 54–66.

2 MATHIESSEN, Peter and George PLIMPTON. "The Art of Fiction, V: An Interview with William Styron." *ParisR*, no. 5 (1954), 42–57. Repr. in 13.3.

3 MC NAMARA, Eugene. "William Styron's *Long March:* Absurdity and Authority." *WHR*, XV (1961), 267–272.

4 MOORE, L. Hugh. "Robert Penn Warren, William Styron, and the Use of Greek Myth." *Crit*, VIII, ii (1966), 75–87.

5 MUDRICK, Marvin. "Mailer and Styron: Guests of the Establishment." *HudR*, XVII (1964), 346–366.

6 O'CONNELL, Shaun. "Expense of Spirit: The Vision of William Styron." *Crit*, VIII, ii (1966), 20–33.

7 O'CONNOR, William Van. "John Updike and William Styron: The Burden of Talent." See 13.12.

8 ROBB, Kenneth A. "William Styron's Don Juan." *Crit*, VIII, ii (1966), 34–46. [On *Set This House on Fire*.]

9 RUBIN, Louis D., Jr. "William Styron: Notes on a Southern Writer in Our Time." See 7.2.

10 STEVENSON, David L. "Styron and the Fiction of the Fifties." *Crit*, III, iii (1960), 47–58. Also in 14.10.

11 URANG, Gunnar. "The Broader Vision: William Styron's *Set This House on Fire*." *Crit*, VIII, ii (1966), 47–69.

Tarkington, Booth (1869–1946)

BIBLIOGRAPHY

12 CURRIE, Barton. *Booth Tarkington: A Bibliography*. Garden City, N.Y.: Doubleday, Doran, 1932.

13 RUSSO, Dorothy Ritter and Thelma L. SULLIVAN. *A Bibliography of Booth Tarkington, 1869–1946*. Indianapolis: Indiana Historical Society, 1949.

14 WAINWRIGHT, Alexander. "Additions to the Tarkington Bibliography." *PULC*, XVI (1955), 89–94.

15 WOODRESS, James. "The Tarkington Papers." *PULC*, XVI (1955), 45–53. [A description of the Princeton Library collection.]

BIOGRAPHICAL AND CRITICAL BOOKS

16 WOODRESS, James. *Booth Tarkington: Gentlemen from Indiana*. Philadelphia: Lippincott, 1955. [Biography.]

BIOGRAPHICAL AND CRITICAL ESSAYS

1 BOYNTON, Percy H. "Booth Tarkington." *EJ*, XII (1923), 117–125.

2 COOPER, Frederic Taber. *Some American Story Tellers*. New York: Holt, 1911, 196–224.

3 QUINN, Arthur Hobson. "Booth Tarkington and the Later Romance." See 4.11.

4 SCOTT, Winfield Townley. "Tarkington and the 1920's." *ASch*, XXVI (1957), 181–194.

5 SEELYE, John D. "That Marvelous Boy—Penrod Once Again." *VQR*, XXXVII (1960), 591–604.

6 SHERMAN, Stuart Pratt. "Mr. Tarkington on the Midland Personality." *Points of View*. New York: Scribner, 1924, 229–233.

7 VAN DOREN, Carl. "Booth Tarkington." See 7.5.

8 WOODRESS, James. "Booth Tarkington's Political Career." *AL*, XXVI (1954), 209–222.

9 WYATT, Edith Franklin. "Booth Tarkington: The Seven Ages of Man." *NAR*, CCXVI (1922), 499–512.

Updike, John (1932–)

BIOGRAPHICAL AND CRITICAL ESSAYS

10 BRENNER, Gerry. "*Rabbit, Run:* John Updike's Criticism of the 'Return to Nature'." *TCL*, XII (1966), 3–14.

11 DETWEILER, Robert. "John Updike and the Indictment of Culture-Protestantism." *Spiritual Crises in Mid-Century American Fiction*. Gainesville, Fla.: Univ. of Florida Press, 1964, 14–24.

12 DONER, Dean. "Rabbit Angstrom's Unseen World." *New World Writing*, No. 20 (1962), 58–75. [On *Rabbit, Run*.]

13 DOYLE, P. A. "Updike's Fiction: Motifs and Techniques." *CathW*, CXCIX (1964), 356–362.

14 GALLOWAY, David D. "The Absurd Man as Saint: The Novels of John Updike." *MFS*, X (1964), 111–127. Also in 9.5.

15 HICKS, Granville. See 12.17.

16 MIZENER, Arthur. "The American Hero as High-School Boy." See 13.11.

17 MURADIAN, Thaddeus. "The World of Updike." *EJ*, LIV (1965), 577–584.

18 O'CONNOR, William Van. "John Updike and William Styron: The Burden of Talent." See 13.12.

19 RUPP, Richard H. "John Updike: Style in Search of A Center." *SR*, LXXV (1967), 693–709.

20 STANDLEY, Fred L. "*Rabbit, Run:* An Image of Life." *MQ*, VIII (1967), 371–386.

1 TATE, Sister Judith M. "John Updike: Of Rabbits and Centaurs." *Critic*, XXII (1964), 44–51.

2 WARD, J. A. "John Updike's Fiction." *Crit*, V (1962), 27–40.

3 YATES, Norris W. "The Doubt and Faith of John Updike." *CE*, XXVI (1965), 469–474.

Warren, Robert Penn (1905–)

TEXTS

4 BROOKS, Cleanth and Robert Penn WARREN, eds. *Understanding Fiction.* 3rd ed. New York: Appleton-Century-Crofts, 1960.

5 *Selected Essays.* New York: Random House, 1958. [Includes essays on Faulkner, Hemingway, Wolfe, Welty, K. A. Porter.] [V-347-Vin]

BIBLIOGRAPHY

6 BEEBE, Maurice and Erin MARCUS. "Criticism of Robert Penn Warren: A Selected Checklist." *MFS*, VI (1960), 83–88.

7 STALLMAN, Robert W. "Robert Penn Warren: A Checklist of His Critical Writings." *UKCR*, XIV (1947), 78–83.

BIOGRAPHICAL AND CRITICAL BOOKS

8 BOHNER, Charles H. *Robert Penn Warren.* New York: Twayne, 1964. [T-69-C&UPS]

9 CASPER, Leonard. *Robert Penn Warren: The Dark and Bloody Ground.* Seattle, Wash.: Univ. of Washington Press, 1960. [Includes excellent bibliography.]

10 KALLSEN, Loren J., ed. *The Kentucky Tragedy: A Problem in Romantic Attitudes.* Indianapolis, Ind.: Bobbs-Merrill, 1963. [A collection of documents on the Beauchamp-Sharp murder case of 1825, on which Warren's *World Enough and Time* is based.]

11 LONGLEY, John Lewis, Jr., ed. *Robert Penn Warren: A Collection of Critical Essays.* New York: New York Univ. Press, 1965 (Orig.). [Includes selected bibliography.] [NYU]

12 SOCHATOFF, A Fred and others, eds. *All the King's Men: A Symposium.* Pittsburgh, Pa.: Carnegie Press, 1957.

13 WEST, Paul. *Robert Penn Warren.* UMPAW, No. 44. Minneapolis, Minn.: Univ. of Minnesota Press, 1964. [UMP]

BIOGRAPHICAL AND CRITICAL ESSAYS

1 ANDERSON, Charles Roberts. "Violence and Order in the Novels of Robert Penn Warren." *HoR*, VI (1953), 88–105. Also in 13.9 and 14.4.

2 BAKER, Joseph E. "Irony in Fiction: *All the King's Men*." *CE*, IX (1947), 122–130.

3 BASSO, Hamilton. "The Huey Long Legend." *Life*, XXI (Dec. 9, 1946), 106–108, 110, 112, 115–116, 118–121. [Apropos of *All the King's Men*.]

4 BAUMBACH, Jonathan. "The Metaphysics of Demagoguery: *All the King's Men*." See 5.4.

5 BENTLEY, Eric. "The Meaning of Robert Penn Warren's Novels." *KR*, X (1948), 407–424. Also in 13.15.

6 BERNER, Robert. "The Required Past: *World Enough and Time*." *MFS*, VI (1960), 55–64.

7 BRADBURY, John M. "Robert Penn Warren's Novels: The Symbolic and Textural Patterns." *Accent*, XIII (1953), 77–89. Also in 93.11.

8 CAMPBELL, Harry Modean. "Warren as Philosopher in *World Enough and Time*." *HoR*, VI (1953), 106–116. Also in 14.4.

9 CARGILL, Oscar. "Anatomist of Monsters." *CE*, IX (1947), 1–8.

10 CARTER, Everett. "The 'Little Myth' of Robert Penn Warren." *MFS*, VI (1960), 3–12.

11 CASPER, Leonard. "Journey to the Interior: *The Cave*." *MFS*, VI (1960), 65–72. Also in 93.11.

12 CASPER, Leonard. "Miscegenation as Symbol: *Band of Angels*." See 93.11.

13 CLEMENTS, A. L. "Theme and Reality in *At Heaven's Gate* and *All the King's Men*." *Criticism*, V (1963), 27–44.

14 DAVIS, Joe. "Robert Penn Warren and the Journey to the West." *MFS*, VI (1960), 73–82.

15 DOUGLAS, Wallace W. "Drug Store Gothic: The Style of Robert Penn Warren." *CE*, XV (1954), 265–272.

16 FLINT, F. Cudworth. "Mr. Warren and the Reviewers." *SR*, LXIV (1956), 632–645. Also in 93.11. [Review-article dealing with *Band of Angels*.]

17 FRANK, Joseph. "Romanticism and Reality in Robert Penn Warren." *HudR*, IV (1951), 248–258.

18 GIRAULT, N. R. "The Narrator's Mind as Symbol: An Analysis of *All the King's Men*." *Accent*, VII (1947), 220–234.

19 HARDY, John Edward. "Robert Penn Warren's Double Hero." *VQR*, XXXVI (1960), 583–597.

20 HAVARD, William C. "The Burden of the Literary Mind: Some Meditations on Robert Penn Warren as Historian." *SAQ*, LXII (1963), 516–531. Also in 93.11.

1 HEILMAN, Robert B. "Melpomene as Wallflower; or, The Reading of Tragedy." *SR*, LV (1947), 154–166. Also in 93.11. [Survey of criticism of *All the King's Men*.]

2 HEILMAN, Robert B. "Tangled Web." *SR*, LIX (1951), 107–119. Also in 93.11. [Essay-review of *World Enough and Time*.]

3 HENDRY, Irene. "The Regional Novel: The Example of Robert Penn Warren." *SR*, LIII (1945), 84–102.

4 HYNES, Samuel. "Robert Penn Warren: The Symbolic Journey." *UKCR*, XVII (1951), 279–285.

5 JONES, Madison. "The Novels of Robert Penn Warren." *SAQ*, LXII (1963), 488–498.

6 JOOST, Nicholas. " 'Was All for Naught?': Robert Penn Warren and New Directions in the Novel." See 13.4.

7 JUSTUS, James H. "The Uses of Gesture in Warren's *The Cave*." *MLQ*, XXVI (1965), 448–461.

8 JUSTUS, James H. "Warren's *World Enough and Time* and *Beauchamp's Confession*." *AL*, XXXIII (1962), 500–511.

9 KELVIN, Norman. "The Failure of Robert Penn Warren." *CE*, XVIII (1957), 355–364.

10 KERR, Elizabeth M. "Polarity of Themes in *All the King's Men*." *MFS*, VI (1960), 25–46.

11 KING, Roma A., Jr. "Time and Structure in the Early Novels of Robert Penn Warren." *SAQ*, LVI (1957), 486–493.

12 LETARGEEZ, J. "Robert Penn Warren's View of History." *RLV*, XXII (1956), 533–543.

13 LONGLEY, John Lewis, Jr. "*At Heaven's Gate:* The Major Themes." *MFS*, VI (1960), 13–24. Also in 93.11.

14 LONGLEY, John Lewis, Jr. "When All Is Said and Done: Warren's *Flood*." See 93.11.

15 MARTIN, Terence. "*Band of Angels:* The Definition of Self-definition." *Folio*, XXI (1955), 31–37.

16 MC DOWELL, Frederick P. "Robert Penn Warren's Criticism." *Accent*, XV (1955), 173–196. [Includes a selective bibliography of Warren's criticism.]

17 MC DOWELL, Frederick P. W. "The Romantic Tragedy of Self in *World Enough and Time*." *Crit*, I (1957), 34–48. Also in 93.11.

18 *Modern Fiction Studies*, VI (1960). Robert Penn Warren Special Number. [Seven essays, plus a bibliography of reviews and criticism.]

19 MOHRT, Michel. "Robert Penn Warren and the Myth of the Outlaw." *YFS*, No. 10 (1953), 70–84.

20 MOORE, L. Hugh. "Robert Penn Warren, William Styron, and the Use of Greek Myth." *Crit*, VIII, ii (1966), 75–87.

21 RATHBUN, John W. "Philosophy, *World Enough and Time*, and the Art of the Novel." *MFS*, VI (1960), 47–54.

22 RUBIN, Louis D., Jr. "All the King's Meanings." *GaR*, VIII (1954), 422–434.

1 ROUFF, James. "Humpty Dumpty and *All the King's Men:* A Note on Robert Penn Warren's Teleology." *TCL*, III (1957), 128–134. Also in 14.11.

2 RYAN, Alvan S. "Robert Penn Warren's *Night Rider:* The Nihilism of the Isolated Temperament." *MFS*, VI (1961), 338–346. Also in 93.11.

3 SILLARS, Malcolm O. "Warren's *All the King's Men:* A Study in Populism." *AQ*, IX (1957), 345–353.

4 STEWART, John L. "Robert Penn Warren and the Knot of History." *ELH*, XXVI (1959), 102–136.

5 STRUGNELL, John R. "Robert Penn Warren and the Uses of the Past." *REL*, IV (1963), 93–102.

6 WARREN, Robert Penn. "*All the King's Men:* The Matrix of Experience." *YR*, LIII (1964), 161–167. Also in 93.11.

7 WASSERSTROM, William. "Robert Penn Warren: From Paleface to Redskin." *PrS*, XXXI (1957), 323–333.

8 WHITE, Ellington, "Robert Penn Warren." See 14.3.

9 WHITE, Robert. "Robert Penn Warren and the Myth of the Garden." *FaS*, III (1954), 59–67.

Welty, Eudora (1909–   )

BIBLIOGRAPHY

10 GROSS, Seymour L. "Eudora Welty: A Bibliography of Criticism and Comment." *Sec.'s News Sheet*, Bibliog. Soc., Univ. of Va., No. 45 (1960), 1–32.

11 SMYTHE, Katherine H. "Eudora Welty: A Checklist." *BB*, XXI (1956), 207–208.

BIOGRAPHICAL AND CRITICAL BOOKS

12 APPEL, Alfred, Jr. *A Season of Dreams: The Fiction of Eudora Welty* Baton Rouge, La.: Louisiana State Univ. Press, 1965.

13 KIEFT, Ruth M. Vande. *Eudora Welty.* New York: Twayne, 1962. [T-15-C&UPS]

BIOGRAPHICAL AND CRITICAL ESSAYS

14 DANIEL, Robert W. "Eudora Welty: The Sense of Place." See 14.3.

15 DANIEL, Robert. "The World of Eudora Welty." *HoR*, VI (1953), 49–58. Also in 14.4.

16 DRAKE, Robert Y. "The Reasons of the Heart." *GaR*, XI (1957), 420–426. [Compares *The Ponder Heart* with the stage adaptation.]

1 FELHEIM, Marvin. "Eudora Welty and Carson McCullers." See 13.12.

2 GLENN, Eunice. "Fantasy in the Fiction of Eudora Welty." *A Southern Vanguard*. Ed. by Allen Tate. New York: Prentice-Hall, 1947, 78–91. Also in 12.14.

3 HARDY, John Edward. "*Delta Wedding* as Region and Symbol." *SR*, LX (1952), 397–418.

4 HICKS, Granville. "Eudora Welty." *CE*, XIV (1952), 69–76; *EJ*, XLI (1952), 461–468.

5 HOLLAND, Robert B. "Dialogue as a Reflection of Place in *The Ponder Heart*." *AL*, XXXV (1963), 352–358.

6 JONES, Alun R. "The World of Love: The Fiction of Eudora Welty." See 12.17.

7 JONES, William M. "Name and Symbol in the Prose of Eudora Welty." *SFQ*, XXII (1958), 173–185.

8 KIEFT, Ruth M. Vande. "The Mysteries of Eudora Welty." *GaR*, XV (1961), 343–357.

9 MORRIS, Harry C. "Eudora Welty's Use of Mythology." *Shenandoah*, VI (1955), 34–40.

10 MORRIS, Harry C. "Zeus and the Golden Apples: Eudora Welty." *Perspectives USA*, V (1953), 190–199. [Myth in *The Golden Apples*.]

11 OPITZ, Kurt. "Eudora Welty: The Order of a Captive Soul." *Crit*, VII, ii (1965), 79–91.

12 PORTER, Katherine Anne. "Eudora Welty and 'A Curtain of Green'." *The Days Before*. New York: Harcourt, Brace, 1952, 101–115. [Partly biographical.]

13 RANSOM, John Crowe. "Delta Fiction." *KR*, VIII (1946), 503–507. [On *Delta Wedding*.]

14 RUBIN, Louis D., Jr. "The Golden Apples of the Sun." See 7.2. [On *Delta Wedding* and *The Golden Apples*.]

15 VAN GELDER, Robert. "An Interview with Eudora Welty." See 14.9.

16 WARREN, Robert Penn. "The Love and Separateness in Miss Welty." *KR*, VI (1944), 246–259. Also in 93.5.

17 WELTY, Eudora. "How I Write." *VQR*, XXXI (1955), 240–251. Also in 93.4.

18 WELTY, Eudora. "Place in Fiction." *SAQ*, LV (1956), 57–72. Repr. as *Place in Fiction*. New York: House of Books, Ltd., 1957.

19 WELTY, Eudora. "The Reading and Writing of Short Stories." *Atlantic*, CLXXXIII (Mar., 1949), 54–58; (Feb.), 46–49.

20 WELTY, Eudora. "Words into Fiction." *SoR*, I (1965), 543–553.

21 WEST, Ray B., Jr. "Three Methods of Modern Fiction: Ernest Hemingway, Thomas Mann, Eudora Welty." *CE*, XII (1951), 193–203.

Wescott, Glenway (1901–   )

BIBLIOGRAPHY

1 KAHN, Sy M. "Glenway Wescott: A Bibliography." *BB*, XXII (1958), 156–160.

BIOGRAPHICAL AND CRITICAL BOOKS

2 RUECKERT, William H. *Glenway Wescott.* New York: Twayne, 1965. [T-87-C&UPS]

3 *Images of Truths Remembrances and Criticism.* New York: Harper & Row, 1962. [CN-38-CN]

BIOGRAPHICAL AND CRITICAL ESSAYS

4 BRACE, Marjorie. See 8.1.

5 COWLEY, Malcolm. See 2.8.

6 GALLOS, Stephen. "An Analysis of Wescott's *The Pilgrim Hawk.*" *Crit*, VIII, ii (1966), 13–19.

7 KAHN, Sy. "Glenway Wescott: The Artist at Work." *PELL*, I (1965), 250–258.

8 KOHLER, Dayton. "Glenway Wescott: Legend Maker." *Bookman*, LXXIII (1931), 142–145. [Essay-review on *The Babe's Bed.*]

9 MILLETT, Fred B. "Introduction." *The Grandmothers.* Harper's Modern Classics Edition. New York: Harper, 1950.

10 QUINN, Patrick F. "The Case History of Glenway Wescott." *F&M*, XIX (1939), 11–16.

11 SCHORER, C. E. "The Maturing of Glenway Wescott." *CE*, XVIII (1957), 320–326.

12 ZABEL, Morton Dauwen. "The Whisper of the Hawk." In Zabel, *Craft and Character in Modern Fiction.* New York: Viking, 1957, 304–308. [On *The Pilgrim Hawk.*]

West, Nathanael (1902–1940)

TEXTS

13 ROSS, Alan, ed. *The Complete Works of Nathanael West.* With introd. New York: Farrar, Straus & Cudahy, 1957.

BIBLIOGRAPHY

1 WHITE, William. "Nathanael West: A Bibliography." *SB*, XI (1958), 207–224.

BIOGRAPHICAL AND CRITICAL BOOKS

2 COMERCHERO, Victor. *Nathanael West, The Ironic Prophet.* Syracuse, N.Y.: Syracuse Univ. Press, 1964.

3 HYMAN, Stanley Edgar. *Nathanael West.* UMPAW, No. 21. Minneapolis, Minn.: Univ. of Minnesota Press, 1962. [UMP]

4 LIGHT, James F. *Nathanael West: An Interpretative Study.* Evanston, Ill.: Northwestern Univ. Press, 1961.

5 REID, Randall. *The Fiction of Nathanael West: No Redeemer, No Promised Land.* Chicago, Ill.: Univ. of Chicago Press, 1967.

BIOGRAPHICAL AND CRITICAL ESSAYS

6 AARON, Daniel. "The Truly Monstrous: A Note on Nathanael West." *PR*, XIV (1947), 98–106.

7 ANDREACH, Robert J. "Nathanael West's *Miss Lonelyhearts* Between the Dead Pan and the Unborn Christ." *MFS*, XII (1966), 251–260.

8 COATES, Robert M. Introduction. *Miss Lonelyhearts.* New York: New Directions, 1946, 1–7; 1950, ix–xiv.

9 COLLINS, Carvel. "Nathanael West's *The Day of the Locust* and *Sanctuary*." *FaS*, II (Summer, 1953), 23–24.

10 DANIEL, Carter A. "West's Revisions of *Miss Lonelyhearts*." *SB*, XVI (1963), 232–243.

11 GALLOWAY, David D. "Nathanael West's Dream Dump." *Crit*, VI, iii (1963), 46–64.

12 GALLOWAY, David D. "A Picaresque Apprenticeship: Nathanael West's *The Dream Life of Balso Snell* and *A Cool Million*." *WSCL*, V (1964), 110–126

13 GEHMAN, Richard B. Introduction. *The Day of the Locust.* New York: New Directions, 1950, ix–xxiii.

14 GILMORE, T. B. "Dark Night of the Cave: Rejoinder to [Alvin] Kernan on *Day of the Locust*." *SNL*, II (1964), 95–100.

15 HERBST, Josephine. "Nathanael West." *KR*, XXIII (1961), 611–630.

16 HOLLIS, C. Carroll. "Nathanael West and the 'Lonely Crowd'." *Thought*, XXXIII (1958), 398–416.

17 KERNAN, Alvin. "The Mob Tendency in Satire: *The Day of the Locust*." *SNL*, I (1963), 11–20.

18 LIGHT, James F. "*Miss Lonelyhearts:* The Imagery of Nightmare." *AQ*, VIII (1956), 316–327.

19 LIGHT, James F. "Nathanael West and the Ravaging Locust." *AQ*, XII (1960), 44–54.

1 LIGHT, James F. "Nathanael West, 'Balso Snell,' and the Mundane Mill-stone." *MFS*, IV (1958), 319–328.

2 LOKKE, V. L. "A Side Glance at Medusa: Hollywood, the Literature Boys, and Nathanael West." *SWR*, XLVI (1961), 35–45.

3 LORCH, Thomas M. "The Inverted Structure of *Balso Snell*." *SSF*, IV (1966), 33–41.

4 LORCH, Thomas M. "West's *Miss Lonelyhearts:* Skepticism Mitigated?" *Renascence*, XVIII (1966), 99–109.

5 PRITCHETT, V. S. "Miss Lonelyhearts." *The Living Novel and Later Appreciations*. New York: Random House, 1964, 76–82.

6 RATNER, Marc L. "Anywhere Out of This World: Baudelaire and Nathanael West." *AL*, XXXI (1960), 456–463.

7 ROSS, Alan. "The Dead Centre: An Introduction to Nathanael West." *Horizon*, XVIII (1948), 284–296. Repr. in 98.13.

8 SCHWARTZ, Edward Greenfield. "The Novels of Nathanael West." *Accent*, XVII (1957), 251–262. [A review-article.]

9 TIBBETTS, A. M. "The Strange Half-World of Nathanael West." *PrS*, XXXIV (1960), 8–14.

10 VOLPE, Edmond L. "The Waste Land of Nathanael West." *Renascence*, XIII (1961), 69–77, 112.

Wilder, Thornton (1897–)

BIBLIOGRAPHY

11 BRYER, Jackson R. "Thornton Wilder and the Reviewers." *PBSA*, LVIII (1964), 35–49. [Checklist of critiques.]

12 EDELSTEIN, J. M., comp. *A Bibliographical Checklist of the Writings of Thornton Wilder*. New Haven, Conn.: Yale University Press, 1959.

13 KOSOK, Heinz. "Thornton Wilder: A Bibliography of Criticism." *TCL*, IX (1963), 93–100.

BIOGRAPHICAL AND CRITICAL BOOKS

14 BURBANK, Rex. *Thornton Wilder*. New York: Twayne, 1961. [T-5-C&UPS]

15 GOLDSTEIN, Malcolm. *The Art of Thornton Wilder*. Lincoln, Nebr.: Univ. of Nebraska Press, 1965. [BB-308-Bison]

16 GREBANIER, Bernard. *Thornton Wilder*. UMPAW, No. 34. Minneapolis, Minn.: Univ. of Minnesota Press, 1964. [UMP]

BIOGRAPHICAL AND CRITICAL ESSAYS

17 BLACKMUR, R. P. "Thornton Wilder." *H&H*, III (1930), 586–589.

1 BROWN, E. K. "A Christian Humanist: Thornton Wilder." *UTQ*, IV (1935), 356–370.

2 COWIE, Alexander. "The Bridge of Thornton Wilder." *Essays on American Literature in Honor of Jay B. Hubbell*. Ed. by Clarence Gohdes. Durham, N.C.: Duke Univ. Press, 1967, 307–328.

3 COWLEY, Malcolm. Introduction to *A Thornton Wilder Trio*. New York: Criterion Books, 1956.

4 FIREBAUGH, Joseph J. "The Humanism of Thornton Wilder." *PS*, IV (1950), 426–438.

5 *Four Quarters*, XVI, iv (May, 1967). Thornton Wilder Number. (Six essays by various hands.)

6 FULLER, Edmund. "Thornton Wilder: The Notation of the Heart." *ASch*, XXVIII (1959), 210–217.

7 GARDNER, Martin. "Thornton Wilder and the Problem of Providence." *UR*, VII (1940), 83–91.

8 GOLD, Michael. "Thornton Wilder: Prophet of the Genteel Christ." *NewR*, LXIV (Oct. 22, 1930), 266–267.

9 GOLDSTONE, Richard H. "The Art of Fiction XVI: Thornton Wilder." *ParisR*, No. 15 (1957), 37–57.

10 GREENE, George. "The World of Thornton Wilder." *Thought*, XXXVII (1962), 563–584.

11 KOHLER, Dayton. "Thornton Wilder." *EJ*, XXVIII (1939), 1–11.

12 WESCOTT, Glenway. "Talks with Thornton Wilder." *Images of Truth: Remembrances and Criticism*. New York: Harper & Row, 1962, 242–308.

13 WILSON, Edmund. "Thornton Wilder: The Influence of Proust." *NewR*, LV (Aug. 8, 1928), 303–305.

Wolfe, Thomas (1900–1938)

TEXTS

14 BRASWELL, William and Leslie A. FIELD, eds. *Thomas Wolfe's Purdue Speech, "Writing and Living," Edited from the Dictated and Revised Transcript*. Lafayette, Ind.: Purdue Univ. Studies, 1964.

15 CARGILL, Oscar and Thomas C. POLLOCK, eds. *The Correspondence of Thomas Wolfe and Homer Andrew Watt*. New York: New York Univ. Press, 1954. [Correspondence between Wolfe and the Chairman of the English Department at NYU.]

16 GEISMAR, Maxwell, ed. *The Portable Thomas Wolfe*. New York: Viking, 1946.

17 HOLMAN, C. Hugh, ed. *The Short Novels of Thomas Wolfe*. With introd. and head-notes. New York: Scribner, 1961.

18 HOLMAN, C. Hugh, ed. *The Thomas Wolfe Reader*. With introd. New York: Scribner, 1964. [Scrib]

19 NOWELL, Elizabeth, ed. *The Letters of Thomas Wolfe*. New York: Scribner, 1956.

20 TERRY, John Skally, ed. *Thomas Wolfe's Letters to His Mother*. New York: Scribner, 1943.

1 WHEELOCK, John Hall, ed. *Editor to Author: The Letters of Maxwell E. Perkins.* New York: Scribner, 1950.

2 WOLFE, Thomas. *The Story of A Novel.* New York: Scribner, 1936.

BIBLIOGRAPHY

3 BEEBE, Maurice and Leslie A. FIELD. "Criticism of Thomas Wolfe: A Selected Checklist." *MFS*, XI (1965), 315–328.

4 HOLMAN, C. Hugh. "Thomas Wolfe: A Bibliographical Study." *TSLL*, I (1959), 427–445.

5 JOHNSON, Elmer D. *Of Time and Thomas Wolfe: A Bibliography with a Character Index of His Works.* New York: Scarecrow Press, 1959.

6 KAUFFMAN, Beatrice. "Bibliography of Periodical Articles on Thomas Wolfe." *BB*, XVII (1942), 162–165, 172–190.

7 LITTLE, Thomas. "The Thomas Wolfe Collection of William B. Wisdom." *HLB*, I (1947), 280–287.

8 PRESTON, George R., Jr. *Thomas Wolfe: A Bibliography.* New York: Charles S. Boesen, 1943.

9 THOMPSON, Betty. "Thomas Wolfe: Two Decades of Criticism." *SAQ*, XLIX (1950), 378–392.

10 WAINWRIGHT, Alexander D. Review of Elmer D. Johnson, *Of Time and Thomas Wolfe. PBSA*, LV (1961), 258–263. [Additions to and corrections of Johnson's work.]

BIOGRAPHICAL AND CRITICAL BOOKS

11 ADAMS, Agatha Boyd. *Thomas Wolfe: Carolina Student.* Chapel Hill, N.C.: Univ. of North Carolina Library, 1950.

12 BRODIN, Pierre. *Thomas Wolfe.* Trans. by Imogene Riddick with introd. by Richard Walser. Asheville, N.C.: The Stephens Press, 1949.

13 DANIELS, Jonathan. *Thomas Wolfe: October Recollections.* Columbia, S.C.: Bostick and Thornley, 1961. [A pamphlet.]

14 HOLMAN, C. Hugh. *Thomas Wolfe.* UMPAW, No. 6. Minneapolis, Minn.: Univ. of Minnesota Press, 1960. [UMP]

15 JOHNSON, Pamela Hansford. *Hungry Gulliver: An English Critical Appraisal of Thomas Wolfe.* New York: Scribner, 1948.

16 KENNEDY, Richard S. *The Window of Memory: The Literary Career of Thomas Wolfe.* Chapel Hill, N.C.: Univ. of North Carolina Press, 1962.

17 MC ELDERRY, Bruce R., Jr. *Thomas Wolfe.* New York: Twayne, 1964. [T-50-C&UPS]

18 MULLER, Herbert J. *Thomas Wolfe.* Norfolk, Conn.: New Directions, 1947.

19 NORWOOD, Hayden. *The Marble Man's Wife: Thomas Wolfe's Mother.* New York: Scribner, 1947.

20 NOWELL, Elizabeth. *Thomas Wolfe: A Biography.* Garden City, N.Y.: Doubleday, 1960.

1 POLLOCK, Thomas Clark and Oscar CARGILL. *Thomas Wolfe at Washington Square.* New York: New York Univ. Press, 1954.

2 RAYNOLDS, Robert. *Thomas Wolfe: Memoir of a Friendship.* Austin, Tex.: Univ. of Texas Press, 1965.

3 RUBIN, Louis D., Jr. *Thomas Wolfe: The Weather of His Youth.* Baton Rouge, La.: Louisiana State Univ. Press, 1955.

4 WALSER, Richard, ed. *The Enigma of Thomas Wolfe: Biographical and Critical Selections.* Cambridge Mass: Harvard Univ. Press, 1953. [Essays by various hands.]

5 WALSER, Richard. *Thomas Wolfe: An Introduction and Interpretation.* New York: Holt, Rinehart & Winston, 1961.

6 WATKINS, Floyd C. *Thomas Wolfe's Characters: Portraits from Life* Norman, Okla.: Univ. of Oklahoma Press, 1957.

7 WHEATON, Mabel Wolfe, with LeGette BLYTHE. *Thomas Wolfe and His Family.* Garden City, N.Y.: Doubleday, 1961. [Memoir by Wolfe's sister.]

BIOGRAPHICAL AND CRITICAL ESSAYS

8 ALBRECHT, W. P. "Time as Unity in the Novels of Thomas Wolfe." *NMQR*, XIX (1949), 320–329. Also in 103.4.

9 ARMSTRONG, A. W. "As I Saw Thomas Wolfe." *ArQ*, II (1946), 5–14.

10 BAKER, Carlos. "Thomas Wolfe's Apprenticeship." *DQ*, XXIII (1940), 20–25.

11 BASSO, Hamilton. "Thomas Wolfe, A Portrait." *NewR*, LXXXVII (June 24, 1936), 199–202. Also in 13.2.

12 BATES, Ernest Sutherland. "Thomas Wolfe." *EJ*, XXVI (1937), 519–527.

13 BEACH, Joseph Warren. "Thomas Wolfe: The Search for a Father" and "Thomas Wolfe: Discovery of Brotherhood." See 5.5.

14 BEJA, Morris. "Why You Can't Go Home Again: Thomas Wolfe and 'The Escapes of Time and Memory'." *MFS*, XI (1965), 297–314.

15 BELL, Alladine. "T. Wolfe of 10 Montague Terrace." *AR*, XX (1960), 315–330.

16 BISHOP, John Peale. "The Sorrows of Thomas Wolfe." *KR*, I (1939), 7–17. Also in 12.14 and 13.9.

17 BOWDEN, Edwin T. See 7.19.

18 BOYLE, Thomas E. "Thomas Wolfe: Theme Through Imagery." *MFS*, XI (1965), 259–268.

19 BOYNTON, Percy H. See 5.7.

20 BROWN, E. K. "Thomas Wolfe: Realist and Symbolist." *UTQ*, X (1941), 153–166. Also in 103.4.

21 BUDD, Louis J. "The Grotesques of Anderson and Wolfe." *MFS*, V (1959), 304–310.

1 BURGUM, Edwin Berry. "Thomas Wolfe's Discovery of America." *VQR*, XXII (1946), 421–437. Also in 8.4 and 103.4.

2 BURLINGAME, Roger. *Of Making Many Books*. New York: Scribner, 1946, 40–42, 169–190, 324–326.

3 CARGILL, Oscar. "Gargantua Fills His Skin." *UKCR*, XVI (1949), 20–30.

4 CARPENTER, Frederic Ives. "Thomas Wolfe: The Autobiography of an Idea." *UKCR*, XII (1946), 179–188.

5 CHITTICK, V. L. O. "Tom Wolfe's Farthest West." *SWR*, XLVIII (1963), 93–110.

6 CHURCH, Margaret. "Thomas Wolfe: Dark Time." *PMLA*, LXIV (1949), 629–638. Also in 103.4. [Concepts of time in Wolfe and Proust.]

7 CLEMENTS, Clyde C. "Symbolic Patterns in *You Can't Go Home Again*." *MFS*, XI (1965), 286–296.

8 COLLINS, Thomas L. "Thomas Wolfe." *SR*, L (1942), 487–504. Also in 103.4.

9 COWLEY, Malcolm. "Thomas Wolfe." *Atlantic*, CC (Nov., 1957), 202–212.

10 DANIELS, Jonathan. "Poet of the Boom." *Tar Heels*. New York: Dodd, Mead, 1941, 218–235. Also in 103.4.

11 DEVOTO, Bernard. "Genius Is Not Enough." *SatRL*, XIII (Apr. 25, 1936), 3–4, 14–15. Also in 103.4.

12 EATON, Clement. "Student Days with Thomas Wolfe." *GaR*, XVII (1963), 146–155.

13 FALK, Robert. "Thomas Wolfe and the Critics." *CE*, V (1944), 186–192.

14 FROHOCK, W. M. "Thomas Wolfe: Of Time and Neurosis." *SWR*, XXXIII (1948), 349–360. Also in 9.4 and 103.4.

15 GEISMAR, Maxwell. "Thomas Wolfe." See 13.5.

16 GEISMAR, Maxwell. "Thomas Wolfe: The Hillman and the Furies." *YR*, XXXV (1946), 649–666.

17 GEISMAR, Maxwell. "Thomas Wolfe: The Unfound Door." See 6.1.

18 GELFANT, Blanche. "The City as Symbol." See 9.6. [Wolfe as urban novelist.]

19 GOSSETT, Louise Y. See 6.2.

20 GURKO, Leo. *The Angry Decade*. New York: Dodd, Mead, 1947, 148–170.

21 HAWTHORNE, Mark D. "Thomas Wolfe's Use of the Poetic Fragment." *MFS*, XI (1965), 234–244.

22 HOLMAN, C. Hugh. " 'The Dark, Ruined Helen of His Blood': Thomas Wolfe and the South." See 14.3.

23 HOLMAN, C. Hugh. "Thomas Wolfe and the Stigma of Autobiography." *VQR*, XL (1964), 614–625.

24 KAZIN, Alfred. "The Rhetoric and the Agony." See 2.12.

25 KENNEDY, Richard S. "Thomas Wolfe at Harvard, 1920–1923." *HLB*, IV (1950), 172–190, 304–319.

1 KENNEDY, Richard S. "Thomas Wolfe's Don Quixote." *CE*, XXIII (1961), 185–191. [On *The Web and the Rock*.]

2 KENNEDY, Richard S. "Wolfe's *Look Homeward, Angel* as a Novel of Development." *SAQ*, LXIII (1964), 218–226.

3 KENNEDY, Richard S. "Thomas Wolfe and the American Experience." *MFS*, XI (1965), 219–232.

4 KENNEDY, William F. "Economic Ideas in Contemporary Literature: The Novels of Thomas Wolfe." *SEJ*, XX (July, 1953), 35–50.

5 KOHLER, Dayton. "Thomas Wolfe: Prodigal and Lost." *CE*, I (1939), 1–10.

6 KUSSY, Bella. "The Vitalist Trend and Thomas Wolfe." *SR*, L (1942), 306–323.

7 LEDIG-ROWOHLT, H. M. "Thomas Wolfe in Berlin." *ASch*, XXII (1953), 185–201.

8 LOGGINS, Vernon. "Dominant Primordial." See 2.13.

9 MACLACHLAN, J. M. "Folk Concepts in the Novels of Thomas Wolfe." *SFQ*, IX (1945), 175–186.

10 MARTIN, F. David. "The Artist, Autobiography, and Thomas Wolfe." *BuR*, V (1955), 15–28.

11 MC COY, George W. "Asheville and Thomas Wolfe." *NCHR*, XXX (1953), 200–217.

12 MC DOWELL, David. "The Renaissance of Thomas Wolfe." *SR*, LVI (1948), 536–544.

13 MC ELDERRY, B. R., Jr. "The Autobiographical Problem in Thomas Wolfe's Earlier Novels." *ArQ*, IV (1948), 315–324.

14 MEYERHOFF, Hans. "Death of a Genius: The Last Days of Thomas Wolfe." *Commentary*, XIII (Jan., 1952), 44–51.

15 *Modern Fiction Studies*, XI, iii (Autumn, 1965). Thomas Wolfe Number. [Essays by various hands.]

16 MORRIS, Wright. "The Function of Appetite: Thomas Wolfe." See 13.14.

17 MOSER, Thomas C. "Thomas Wolfe, *Look Homeward, Angel*." See 14.7.

18 NORWOOD, Hayden. "Julia Wolfe: Web of Memory." *VQR*, XX (1944), 236–250.

19 PERKINS, Maxwell E. "Thomas Wolfe." *HLB*, I (1947), 269–277. [Reminiscences of Wolfe's editor.]

20 PUSEY, W. W., III. "The German Vogue of Thomas Wolfe." *GR*, XXIII (1948), 131–148.

21 REAVER, J. Russell and Robert I. STROZIER. "Thomas Wolfe and Death." *GaR*, XVI (1962), 330–337. Also in 14.11.

22 ROTHMAN, Nathan L. "Thomas Wolfe and James Joyce: A Study in Literary Influence." *Southern Vanguard*. Ed. by Allen Tate. New York: Prentice-Hall, 1947. Also in 103.4.

1 RUBIN, Larry. "Thomas Wolfe and the Lost Paradise." *MFS*, XI (1965), 250–258.

2 RUBIN, Louis D., Jr. "Thomas Wolfe in Time and Place." *HoR*, VI (1953), 117–132. Also in 14.4.

3 RUBIN, Louis D., Jr. "Thomas Wolfe: Time and the South." See 7.2.

4 SIMPSON, Claude M., Jr. "Thomas Wolfe: A Chapter in His Biography." *SWR*, XXV (1940), 308–321.

5 SKIPP, Francis E. "The Editing of *Look Homeward, Angel.*" *PBSA*, LVII (1963), 1–13.

6 SLOCHOWER, Harry. "Cosmic Exile." *No Voice Is Wholly Lost.* New York: Creative Age, 1945, 93–103.

7 SLOYAN, Gerard S. "Thomas Wolfe: A Legend of Man's Youth in His Hunger." See 13.4.

8 SNELL, George. "The Education of Thomas Wolfe." See 4.12.

9 STEARNS, Monroe M. "The Metaphysics of Thomas Wolfe." *CE*, VI (1945), 193–199. Also in 103.4.

10 STEVENS, Virginia. "Thomas Wolfe's America." *Mainstream*, XI (1958), 1–24.

11 TAYLOR, Walter Fuller. "Thomas Wolfe and the Middle Class Tradition." *SAQ*, LII (1953), 543–554.

12 THORNTON, Mary Lindsay. " 'Dear Mabel': Letters of Thomas Wolfe to His Sister, Mabel Wolfe Wheaton." *SAQ*, LX (1961), 469–483.

13 VAN GELDER, Robert. "Thomas Wolfe as Friends Remember Him." See 14.9.

14 VOGEL, Albert W. "The Education of Eugene Gant." *NMQ*, XXXVI (1966), 278–292.

15 VOLKENING, H. T. "Tom Wolfe: Penance No More." *VQR*, XV (1939), 196–215. Also in 103.1 and 103.4.

16 WALSER, Richard. "Some Notes on Wolfe's Reputation Abroad." *CarQ*, I (1949), 37–48.

17 WARREN, Robert Penn. "A Note on the Hamlet of Thomas Wolfe." *ARev*, V (1935), 191–208. Also in 14.15, 93.5, and 103.4.

18 WATKINS, Floyd C. "Thomas Wolfe and the Nashville Agrarians." *GaR*, VII (1953), 410–423.

19 WATKINS, Floyd C. "Thomas Wolfe's High Sinfulness of Poetry." *MFS*, II (1956), 197–206.

20 WILLIAMS, Cecil B. "Thomas Wolfe Fifteen Years After." *SAQ*, LIV (1955), 523–537.

Wright, Richard (1909–1960)

BIBLIOGRAPHY

1 BRYER, Jackson. "Richard Wright: A Selected Check List of Criticism." *WSCL*, I (1960), 22–33.

2 FABRE, Michel and Edward MARGOLIES. "Richard Wright (1908–1960): A Bibliography." *BB*, XXIV (1965), 131–133, 137.

3 SPRAGUE, M. D. "Richard Wright: A Bibliography." *BB*, XXI (1953), 39.

BIOGRAPHICAL AND CRITICAL BOOKS

4 WEBB, Constance. *Richard Wright: A Biography*. New York: Putnam's, 1968.

BIOGRAPHICAL AND CRITICAL ESSAYS

5 BALDWIN, James. "Many Thousands Gone." *PR*, XVIII (1951), 665–680. Repr. in Baldwin, *Notes of a Native Son*. Boston: Beacon Press, 1955, 24–45. [Detailed discussion of *Native Son*.]

6 BALDWIN, James. "Richard Wright." *Encounter*, XVI (1961), 58–60.

7 BONE, Robert A. See 7.18. [On *Native Son*.]

8 BURGUM, Edwin Berry. "The Promise of Democracy in the Fiction of Richard Wright." *S&S*, VII (1943), 338–353. Also in 8.4.

9 BURNS, Ben. "They're Not Uncle Tom's Children." *Reporter*, XIV (Mar. 8, 1956), 21–23. [Wright in Paris, 1953.]

10 CLAYTON, Horace. "Frightened Children of Frightened Parents." *TAY*, XII–XIII (1945), 262–269. [On *Black Boy*.]

11 DAVIS, Arthur P. " 'The Outsider' as a Novel of Race." *MJ*, VII (1955), 320–326.

12 ELLISON, Ralph. "Richard Wright's Blues." *AR*, V (1945), 198–211. [On *Black Boy*.]

13 EMBREE, E. R. "Native Son." *13 Against the Odds*. New York: Viking, 1944, 25–46. [Includes considerable biographical information.]

14 FORD, Nick Aaron. "The Ordeal of Richard Wright." *CE*, XV (1953), 87–94. [On *Native Son* and *The Outsider*.]

15 FRENCH, Warren. *The Social Novel at the End of an Era*. Carbondale and Edwardsville, Ill.: Univ. of Southern Illinois Press, 1966, 171–180. [On *Native Son*.]

16 GLICKSBERG, Charles I. "Existentialism in *The Outsider*." *FQ*, VII (1958), 17–26.

17 GLICKSBERG, Charles I. See 9.7.

18 GLOSTER, Hugh Morris. "Richard Wright." See 9.8.

19 HARRINGTON, Ollie. "The Last Days of Richard Wright." *Ebony*, XVII (Feb., 1961), 83–94.

1 HILL, Herbert *et al.* "Reflections on Richard Wright: A Symposium on an Exiled Native Son." See 10.2.

2 HUGHES, Carl M. See 10.9.

3 KNOX, George. "The Negro Novelist's Sensibility and the Outsider Theme." *WHR*, XI (1957), 137–148. [On *The Outsider* and Ellison's *Invisible Man*.]

4 LEHAN, Richard. See 10.18.

5 LEWIS, Theophilus. "The Saga of Bigger Thomas." *CathW*, CLIII (1941), 201–206.

6 MARCUS, Steven. See 11.4.

7 RIESMAN, David. "Marginality, Conformity, and Insight." *Phylon*, XIV (1953), 245–253. [On *Black Boy*.]

8 SCOTT, Nathan A., Jr. "Search for Beliefs: Richard Wright." *UKCR*, XXIII (1956), 19–24, 131–138. [Emphasis on *Native Son* and *The Outsider*.]

9 SILLEN, Samuel. "The Meaning of Bigger Thomas." *NewM*, XXXV (Apr., 1960), 13–21.

10 SLOCHOWER, Harry. *No Voice is Wholly Lost*. New York: Creative Age, 1945, 87–92. [Discussion of *Native Son*.]

11 SMITH, William Gardner. "Black Boy in France." *Ebony*, VIII (July, 1953), 32–36, 39–42.

12 WEBB, Constance. "What Next for Richard Wright?" *Phylon*, X (1949), 161–166. [Emphasis on *Native Son* and *Black Boy*.]

13 WHITE, Ralph K. "*Black Boy:* A Value Analysis." *JASP*, XLII (1947), 440–461.

14 WIDMER, Kingsley. "The Existential Darkness: Richard Wright's *The Outsider*." *WSCL*, I (1960), 13–21.

15 WRIGHT, Richard and Antonio FRASCONI. "Exchange of Letters." *TAY*, XII (1945), 255–261.

NOTES

INDEX

INDEX

INDEX

INDEX

INDEX

INDEX